£65 00

Experiencing Risk, Spontaneity and Improvisation in Organizational Change

The perspective of complex responsive processes draws on analogies from the complexity sciences, bringing in the essential characteristics of human agents, understood to emerge in social processes of communicative interaction and power relating. The result is a way of thinking about life in organizations that focuses attention on how organizational members cope with the unknown as they perpetually create organizational futures together.

Providing a natural successor to the editors' earlier series *Complexity and Emergence in Organizations*, this series, *Complexity as the Experience of Organizing*, aims to develop this work further by taking very seriously the *experience* of organizational practitioners, and showing how adopting the perspective of complex responsive processes yields deeper insight into practice and so develops that practice.

This book introduces and explores the possible meanings of the idea of 'working live'. It makes sense of the sense-making *experience* itself, drawing attention to the way ideas and concepts emerge 'live' in all conversations in organizations. An appreciation of the open-ended, *improvisational* nature of ongoing human communication becomes key to such an understanding. The chapters explore:

- How various forms of improvisation in social interaction can inform ways of appreciating how those links are forged.
- How these insights can illuminate the challenges of managing, developing and changing organizational practices.

The editors' commentary introduces and contextualizes these experiences as well as drawing out key themes for further research.

Experiencing Risk, Spontaneity and Improvisation in Organizational Change
will be of value to readers looking for reflective accounts of real life
experiences of *working live* in organizations, rather than further prescriptions
of what life in organizations ought to be like.

Patricia Shaw is Associate Director of the Complexity and Management
Centre at the Business School of the University of Hertfordshire and also an
independent consultant. She is one of the editors of the *Complexity and
Emergence in Organizations* series.

Ralph Stacey is Director of the Complexity and Management Centre at the
Business School of the University of Hertfordshire and Director of the
Doctor of Management programme run by the Centre. He is one of the
editors of the *Complexity and Emergence in Organizations* series, and editor
of five books in this series.

Experiencing Risk, Spontaneity and Improvisation in Organizational Change

Working live

Edited by
Patricia Shaw and Ralph Stacey

Routledge
Taylor & Francis Group

LONDON AND NEW YORK

First published 2006
by Routledge
2 Park Square, Milton Park, Abingdon, Oxon OX14 4RN

Simultaneously published in the USA and Canada
by Routledge
270 Madison Ave, New York, NY 10016

Routledge is an imprint of the Taylor & Francis Group

Transferred to Digital Printing 2006

© 2006 Patricia Shaw and Ralph Stacey

Typeset in Times New Roman by
Keystroke, Jacaranda Lodge, Wolverhampton

British Library Cataloguing in Publication Data
A catalogue record for this book is available from the British Library

Library of Congress Cataloging in Publication Data
Experiencing risk, spontaneity and improvisation in organizational
   change : working live /
   Patricia Shaw and Ralph Stacey, [editors].
      p. cm.
Includes bibliographical references and index.
ISBN 0–415–35128–6 (hard cover) – ISBN 0–415–35129–4 (soft cover)
1. Organizational change–Social aspects. 2. Organizational sociology.
3. Work–Social aspects. I. Shaw, Patricia, 1953– II. Stacey, Ralph D.
   HD58.8.E983 2006
      302.3'5–dc22   2005017599

ISBN 0–415–35128–6 (hbk)
ISBN 0–415–35129–4 (pbk)

Contents

Contributors

Preben Friis is Actor and Director at the Dacapo Company, Denmark, which provides consulting support internationally for organizational change. He was awarded the degree of Master of Arts by research from the Master's/Doctorate of Management programme at the University of Hertfordshire.

Henry Larsen is Research Director and Organizational Consultant at the Dacapo Company, Denmark. He was awarded the degree of Doctor of Management at the University of Hertfordshire.

Patricia Shaw is Associate Director of the Complexity and Management Centre and Visiting Professor at the Business School of the University of Hertfordshire and an independent organizational consultant.

Ralph Stacey is Professor of Management, Director of the Complexity and Management Centre and Director of the Doctor of Management research programme at the University of Hertfordshire.

David Walker is a Clinical Psychologist and Group Analyst with some twenty-five years' experience working within the United Kingdom's National Health Service (NHS) as a clinician, supervisor, manager and leader. At the time of writing he was Director of Therapies in a mental health NHS Trust in London. He is currently employed as clinical leader in a therapeutic community in Norway and also works independently as a group analytic psychotherapist and organizational consultant in Norway and the United Kingdom. He was awarded the degree of Doctor of Management at the University of Hertfordshire.

Series preface
Complexity as the Experience of Organizing

*Edited by Ralph Stacey, Douglas Griffin
and Patricia Shaw*

Complexity as the Experience of Organizing is a sequel to the highly successful series *Complexity and Emergence in Organizations* also edited by the editors of this series. The first series has attracted international attention for its development of the theory of complex responsive processes and its implications for those working in organizations. The perspective of complex responsive processes draws on analogies from the complexity sciences, bringing in the essential characteristics of human agents, namely consciousness and self-consciousness, understood to emerge in social processes of communicative interaction, power relating and evaluative choice. The result is a way of thinking about life in organizations that focuses attention on how organizational members cope with the unknown as they perpetually create organizational futures together. This second series aims to develop that work by taking seriously the experience of organizational practitioners, showing how taking the perspective of complex responsive processes yields deeper insight into practice and so develops that practice.

Contributors to the volumes in the series work as leaders, consultants or managers in organizations. The contributors provide narrative accounts of their actual work, addressing questions such as: What does it mean, in ordinary, everyday terms, to lead a large organization? How do leaders learn to lead? What does it mean, in ordinary everyday terms, to consult to managers in an organization? How does the work of the consultant assist managers when the uncertainty is so great that they do not yet know what they are doing? What does executive coaching achieve? What happens in global change programs such as installing competencies, managing diversity and assuring quality? Why do organizations get stuck in repetitive patterns of behaviour? What kinds of change can be facilitated? In considering such questions in terms of their daily experience, the contributors explore how the perspective of complex responsive processes assists them in making sense of their experience and so develop their practices.

The books in the series are addressed to organizational practitioners and academics who are looking for a different way of making sense of their own experience in a rapidly changing world. The books will attract readers looking for reflective accounts of ordinary, everyday life in organizations rather than idealized accounts or further idealized prescriptions.

Other volumes in the series:
A Complexity Perspective on Researching Organizations
Taking experience seriously
Edited by Ralph Stacey and Douglas Griffin

Complexity and the Experience of Leading Organizations
Edited by Douglas Griffin and Ralph Stacey

Experiencing Emergence in Organizations
Local interaction and the emergence of global pattern
Edited by Ralph Stacey

Complexity and the Experience of Managing in Public Sector Organizations
Edited by Ralph Stacey and Douglas Griffin

 # Preface

Over the period 2000–2002, a number of us at the Complexity and Management Centre at the Business School of the University of Hertfordshire published a series of books called *Complexity and Emergence in Organizations*. These books developed a perspective according to which organizations are understood to be ongoing, iterated processes of cooperative and competitive relating between people. We argued that organizations are not systems, but rather the ongoing patterning of interactions between people. Patterns of human interaction produce further patterns of interaction, not some *thing* outside of the interaction. We called this perspective *complex responsive processes of relating*.

Since 2000 some of the authors in the series, together with other Complexity and Management Centre colleagues in association with the Institute of Group Analysis, have been conducting a research programme on organizational change leading to the degrees of Master of Arts by research or Doctor of Management. This is necessarily a part-time programme because the core of the research method (see another volume in this series, *A Complexity Perspective on Researching Organizations: Taking experience seriously*, edited by Ralph Stacey and Douglas Griffin, 2005) involves students taking their own experience seriously. If patterns of human interaction produce nothing but further patterns of human interaction, in the creation of which we are all participating, then there is no *detached* way of understanding organizations from the position of the objective observer. Instead, organizations have to be understood in terms of one's own personal experience of participating with others in the co-creation of the patterns of interaction that are the organization. The students' research is, therefore, their narration of current events they are *involved* in, together with their reflections on themes of particular importance emerging in the stories of their own experience of participation with others. The research stance is, then, one of detached involvement.

The purpose of this volume is to bring together the work of a number of programme participants who have focused their attention on the improvisational nature of organizational activities. The nature of improvisation is explored, bringing to the fore notions of spontaneity, risk-taking and presence in human relating. The anxiety involved in improvisational actions is highlighted and how managers, leaders and others in organizations live with such anxiety is explored. Leadership and management are usually discussed in terms of rational analysis and planning, or in terms of pre-designed visioning and inspiration. The authors in this volume point to how such 'scripted' behaviour is always only an aspect of wider processes of improvisation. The chapters explore the experience of improvisation in the work of consultants and actors from the Danish Dacapo Theatre who use improvisational theatre in their work with organizations and in the work of the leader of a development programme in an NHS Trust in the United Kingdom.

In Chapter 1 Patricia Shaw takes issue with those who argue that there is nothing spontaneous or unpredictable about the actions people in organizations take and that any appearance of the unpredictable and the unplanned is evidence of some mistake made. She contrasts this view of organizational life with a perspective that takes full account of both the predictability and the unpredictability of ordinary, everyday life in organizations. She explores what it means to 'work live', characterizing such 'working live' as the spontaneous responsiveness of people to each other in which they take the risk of being misunderstood. She argues that even when members of organizations follow 'scripts' in 'set-piece' interactions there is always an element of improvisation.

Henry Larsen and Preben Friis work in the Dacapo Theatre Company in Denmark, which provides a form of consultancy to organizations using theatre. In Chapter 2 they explore the literature on the use of theatre in consulting and argue for a form of organizational consulting that is highly improvisational. They argue that this form of consulting actually constitutes organizational change.

In Chapter 3 Henry Larsen explores the role of spontaneity in his work as a consultant to organizations using theatre. He links this to power, which he sees as relational and constitutive of identity, so that organizational change is essentially change in power relations. He argues that working with theatre contributes to change because of its ability to change power relations. Working with fiction makes it possible for people to take more risks with their status.

Preben Friis reflects on his experience as an actor in theatre consulting in Chapter 4. He explores the relationship between fact and fiction and describes how he and his colleagues are moving towards much more improvisational ways of working with theatre in organizations. He argues that this is a logical consequence of how the management of organizations and change is developing. It is his conviction that in their daily lives in organizations, people are faced with the fact that their actions repeatedly turn out to have unexpected meanings as others respond to what they do, not because of some failure in planning or because the strategy was bad, but because this is an essential characteristic of the interaction between interdependent people in a complex organization. The work of change, then, means paying attention to the fact that people find themselves involved in ongoing improvisation.

In Chapter 5 David Walker, a director in the United Kingdom's public health sector, explores leading as a process and what it means to 'lead in the moment'. He examines how leading in the moment, by which he means an improvisational form of leading, is a necessary complement to the work of vision and strategy, and he suggests that the anxiety of leading in the moment often results in avoiding it. He argues that it is through staying within the experience of the now and participating fully in the moment-by-moment movement which is occurring between people that those in leadership roles are best able to become effective. He explores, from his own experience, how staying with the present moment arouses anxiety, which has to be endured for creative movement to occur.

In Chapter 6 Ralph Stacey gives a brief description of the theoretical foundations of the arguments presented in the previous chapters. He describes how the theory of complex responsive processes can be understood as a theory of organizational improvisation.

The questions of central concern in this volume are as follows. What does it mean to improvise in the activities of managing and leading in organizations? How does such improvisational activity incorporate the deliberate planning activities of managers and leaders? Why does improvisation involve taking risks? How do people in organizations live with the anxiety that such risk-taking entails? What are the implications of the patterning of power relations? How does the use of improvisational theatre constitute organizational consulting and organizational change?

Other volumes in this series are also relevant to the questions posed above. The volume *Experiencing Emergence in Organizations: Local interaction and the emergence of global pattern* is concerned with the manner in which people take up global policies in their ordinary, everyday local interactions with each other. This can be understood as processes of improvisation. The volume *Complexity and the Experience of Leading Organizations* presents a complex responsive processes perspective on leadership and points to the social, improvisational nature of leadership. The volume *A Complexity Perspective on Researching Organizations: Taking experience seriously* explores emergent ways of conducting research in organizations which respect the improvisational nature of life in organizations.

1 Introduction: working live

Patricia Shaw

- ◉ **Response to a planned intervention**
- ◉ **Predictability and spontaneity**
- ◉ **Commitment**
- ◉ **The experience of spontaneity and 'working live'**
- ◉ **The emergence of legitimizing explanations**

The subtitle of this book is the phrase 'working live', a shorthand for pointing to the central ideas explored in this volume, so let us start by teasing out its resonances.

The use of the word 'live' can be associated with the development of technology that allowed us to capture and replay social interaction. We could watch and listen to people engaging with each other without being present at the original situation. Cinema meant that 'live' was no longer a redundant descriptor in the phrase 'live theatre', just as the telephone, and then video links, alerted us to the difference that the absence of first visual and then physical/sensory clues makes to our communication. We had to introduce the term 'face to face' to signal what would previously have been taken for granted. So *at first* the metaphor of 'live' emphasizes that people are *literally* present to one another, whether as 'actors' or 'spectators'.

Moving away from performance in the cinema or theatre, television gave us the idea of the 'live' interview as opposed to the transmission of pre-recorded images. This always engendered an extra tingle of excitement because the control of scriptwriters, directors, editors, designers over what might ensue was in abeyance. The unexpected, the unplanned could happen. Compared with a recording honed by rehearsal and subsequent editing in the cutting room, the live broadcast might be more interesting or more boring. So again *at first* another aspect of the 'live' metaphor emphasizes improvisation *rather than* a predetermined script.

If we probe a little further, though, in our everyday lives we must *always* be improvising together. What I mean by this is that despite the ubiquity of our intentions, plans, rehearsals and scripts, all the effort we put into anticipating, what happens next is never a done deal, because we can never completely predict or control even our own response to what is happening, let alone the responses of others. Understanding our *experience* of everyday communication and thus human organizing as a form of ensemble improvisation is an idea that I have introduced in previous writing (Shaw 2002) pointing out how recognizable 'results' emerge in the interplay of intentions and sense-making among multiple players all drawing on a history of social resources. However, although we are always, in this sense, improvising together, our experience can be more or less lively. Often we engage in deeply familiar repertoires of responses to one another that recreate recognizable roles and scenarios in which who we are and what we are doing follow well-worn patterns giving us a sense of stability, security and solid identity in a reliable world. This is essential for the complex cooperations of social life that we have developed, and at the same time it can also lead us to speak of 'deadly routine'. However, our exchanges are never exact repetitions, but rather iterations; there are always tiny differences which may amplify in further iterations, creating significant novelty. As we continuously respond in evolving situations, we may literally 'find ourselves' afresh. This happens as the processes of mutual recognition by which we 'know' who we are and what we are doing reorganize in improvised joint action. The dull meeting may suddenly 'come to life'. Alternatively, a lively discussion may suddenly shift in quality and the work 'goes dead'.

What happens if we take these aspects of our working lives seriously and inquire into what is going on and what the implications may be for appreciating organizational change? In exploring the *experience* of spontaneity and risk as these fluctuate in our ongoing participation in organizational life, we hope to throw light on issues of politics and ethics as these are shifting and being negotiated 'live' in organizational settings. 'Working live' will here mean asking about our participation in the everyday improvisation of human organizing, often as we are literally present together, but, as we shall see, also as we are metaphorically 'present' to immediate circumstances in which distance, absence, histories and anticipated futures are all in play. Since we are trying to notice what is so ubiquitous as to often go unremarked, this volume turns to a particular change praxis, that of practitioners who draw on disciplines and traditions of thought developed in the world of theatre, to support processes of organizational change. How can such work show us more vividly what we are already engaged in together?

First I will turn to how our sensitivity for the theatrical and what we mean by that can affect our responses to one another. In doing this I also want to offer a first glimpse of the themes this volume will take up. I will describe in some detail an apparently small incident and what followed (actual situation disguised). However, note how such a formulation hides the way circumstances come to be seen as constituting an incident *in* what follows, as much as what follows being provoked by a particular set of circumstances. There is no simple causality at work here; rather, meaningfulness is being socially constructed among participants and, in the process, the relations between people are organizing themselves.

Response to a planned intervention

I am working with a group of people all of whom are engaged in a number of different but related projects across a department. The group includes team leaders, team members and departmental heads. We are meeting first thing in the morning for what has become a regular event: talking together without any defined agenda about whatever matters to us before continuing with the work of the day. Typically, as people collect coffee or water and gather papers, there is a buzz of conversations before quiet settles among the group, then a pause swells before someone starts to speak. On this occasion the buzz has hardly died down before one member of the gathering launches into a proposal about how some future work may be organized which he and another member of the group have been talking about. He continues, gesturing towards his ally, who soon joins in to elaborate on their proposal. Less than a couple of minutes have transpired before I am aware of sensing something 'odd'. Almost simultaneously a colleague says: 'I get the impression you have rehearsed this.' Exactly! I recognize my strange sensations in his comment. There are various mutters and exclamations of agreement around the room: 'Your voice was different.' 'It felt unreal.' 'I didn't understand what was going on.' Clearly, many people had experienced something unusual. Yes, Steve, one of the pair, said that he and George had prepared themselves to the point of agreeing that one would begin before the usual chit-chat had quite died down and that the other would come in soon after. They explained, 'We wanted to see if we could develop discussion on the potential projects here rather than by using the bulletin boards as we had begun to do yesterday.' Rather than pick up this aspect of what the two are saying, many people seem most interested in the various responses evoked during those early couple of minutes. Time is given to making sense of this together and this entails making sense of the further feelings and thoughts stirred as this process continues. The term 'incident' becomes appropriate because of the significance afforded to the early experience of 'something different' during the subsequent discussion.

People begin to voice a range of responses to the early moments of the meeting: the person who had first called attention to the 'rehearsed quality' of the two early speakers said he felt offended by some kind of 'misuse' of the meeting; someone else felt confused, not being able to follow or understand what the two speakers were getting at; someone else felt comforted that two people had prepared a joint approach; someone else was amused that the two were 'giving us a little play'. Those who spoke had all perceived something unusual and had responded variously. As they articulated those responses, the meaning they and others were making of what was happening continued to evolve. The range of feelings expressed provoked further responses: was this a light or a serious matter? In what way did all this matter? Someone pointed out that there were always conversations going on in which people developed intentions jointly and severally to bring up some subject at the morning meeting. Were we trying to say that there was something wrong with that? Why not plan and prepare? It was, after all, a way of being productive. Yes, but in this particular setting, another responded, we come to find out what is on our own and others' minds in a spontaneous way and this feels as though it breaches an unspoken trust. Elaborating, another said that usually whoever spoke did not know what response they would receive, whereas this time there was less risk; the speaker knew that there would be a prepared response to his opening gambit. Someone else said that they realized they felt quite angry, tricked or cheated. Someone was reminded of an occasion in which a friend had appeared at his door, been invited in for a cup of coffee and then during the conversation introduced a prepared pitch for a pyramid selling scheme. He had felt that their friendship was being abused in that the meaning of the invitation into his house was suddenly changed without his acquiescence; he had been deceived. Someone else pointed out that whatever they had prepared, the two allies were probably now surprised by the turn of the conversation. Someone wondered what either of the two were making of what had developed, noticing that both had been sitting for a while with smiles on their faces. One announced that he was feeling rather satisfied with what had been provoked by trying something different; the other said that he realized some people were offended and he wanted to acknowledge that, but there had been no malicious intent in their 'intervention'. Some thought that the two guys were impervious to the significance of what was being raised, others felt that too much was being made of this, and a couple of people said that they were beginning to feel angry that what was allowed or not in the work of the group at this meeting was being 'policed'. The atmosphere was alive with tension, feeling and interest, and a number of people said that it felt risky to venture further comments, although they did so.

At one point someone said that what was a really unusual feature of this discussion was that the 'incident' we were exploring was a commonplace of organizational life – 'I'm always in situations where I am aware of the difference between more studied and more spontaneous contributions to communication; the difference is that we rarely call attention to the experience.' After this the conversation took a further reflective turn. What was the difference between a well-intentioned 'experiment', a 'deception', a 'manipulation', a 'difference' in the sense of something unfamiliar, an innovation? Someone recognized that we were actually in the process of negotiating our way 'live' through these issues and their political and ethical ramifications. It was pointed out that it was one of those with more authority in the group who had first expressed himself as being offended. Someone else said that he was feeling that a 'rule' was being created: don't ever do that (whatever 'that' was). Someone noticed that an ideal of the morning gathering as a 'sacred' space of trust and authenticity was being offered. Was this an idealization and with what consequences? Another remarked that we were discussing ethics. What is good intention? He was reminded of a distinction he found interesting between meaning well, doing well and achieving well. Another recalled the films of the director David Mamet and his perennial interest in 'truth' and 'fakery' in human communication. He mentioned a particular film, *The Spanish Prisoner*, in which Mamet explores the language of business and the work of the con artist. He is asking intriguing questions about how we come to trust one another and ourselves, how we develop mutual confidence and what happens when we lose our bearings in this. We are always acting, but when we literally 'act' and lose our spontaneity, we run the risk of losing our potential to recognize ourselves as we engage the recognition of others. An example of the momentary alienation of such experiences was the way several people did not 'recognize' Steve's (the very first speaker's) voice, and Steve admitted that he was aware of sounding strange to himself. Neither the two protagonists nor their initial 'audience' believed in the 'play'; we were not convinced by the communicative activity we were engaged in together.

Predictability and spontaneity

Why have I given so much space to recounting these exchanges? I am suggesting that such a story potentially offers insights into what is relatively undiscussed in many management books devoted to change. The insights are, first, that change in the organization of personal and social identities emerges spontaneously in processes of communicative action, and second, that our experience of ourselves as spontaneous actors is implicated in these processes. I will look at how circumstances such as I have described might be understood by two influential writers. What aspects might they draw attention to and what might they ignore or discount?

Take first Edgar Schein's (1985) influential account of how organizational cultures are formed and how leaders should think about managing cultural change in organizations. He points to critical incidents or marker events in the life of organizational groupings. He proposes that a critical incident is an occasion of shared emotional reaction and raised anxiety. He takes care to explain that 'shared' here does not mean that people feel the same way, but that all have witnessed the behaviour of some members and the responses of others, and all can refer to this later. Such experiences, he claims, define a group at the emotional level, and culture is created in the articulation of what the experience has actually been and what it means. This articulation, if it 'solves' significant issues for the group's continuation, is what Schein identifies as acts of leadership and culture creation. Those incidents that arouse strong feelings and are then definitively dealt with constitute the stories handed down and offered to newcomers to induct them into the group. These bids to make meaning he understands as individually motivated, intentional acts which produce 'group products' of value to the group 'as a whole'. He is adamant that all change is motivated and that although the actual outcome may be a complex interaction of forces unleashed by the different intentions of different actors, it is never unpredictable. 'When we are dealing with social systems there is no such thing as spontaneous change or mutation –

no unpredictable change' (ibid.: 299). Difficulties in seeing the connection between intentions, actions and results occur because we cannot accurately reconstruct complex sequences of interactions. 'When what happens seems unplanned and unpredicted it is because change agents have miscalculated the effects of their action or they may have been unaware of other forces simultaneously acting' (ibid.: 301).

Because Schein understands the small group as a subsystem of a larger system, the organization, his analysis of culture creation at the micro level can be applied to the macro-level system. Individual leaders are advised to develop depth of vision, breadth of experience, detachment and the ability to tolerate uncertainty and conflict so that they are able to perceive issues which threaten the ongoing life of the organization, articulating these in meaningful ways that solve problems for the organization as a whole. In Schein's work, the manager or change agent is encouraged to believe that intentions are clearly motivated, intentions produce actions, actions produce outcomes and meanings are assigned to those outcomes in intentional ways. Complexity, in terms of the multiplicity of intentional actions in play, is acknowledged as obscuring this clarity, but fundamentally this perspective has had a lasting effect in the popularity of managed culture change programmes in organizations. They often disappoint, but the failures are explained in terms of miscalculations and/or lack of full knowledge of what is in play. So Schein might understand my story in these terms: two players miscalculate the effects of their action, which is construed in a way that raises anxiety for the group, requiring clearly motivated acts of individual leadership to give definitive meaning to the experience, thus further elaborating existing norms in the culture. However, he would say that nothing ultimately unpredictable or spontaneous in the way of change is happening here.

Commitment

How might another influential writer who explores action-driven sense-making in organizations, Karl Weick (1995), perceive the story? Possibly he might see an example of people starting a course of action which becomes irrevocable: Steve and George become committed, once begun, to pursuing their agreement to start a discussion about organizing the projects in the way they had planned, perhaps even more so as their attempt provokes strong responses. It is not just Steve and George who become committed; so does one of their colleagues in authority, because he stands by his feelings of anger roused by the 'breach of trust' as he feels it. Then more people become committed by their continuing actions in response, to make meaning of what they are doing. Because their actions follow Kiesler's criteria (1971) of being explicit (clearly visible), public (important people witness) and, once begun, irrevocable (cannot be undone), Weick might see this as 'committed acts in search of an explanation' (1995: 156). He suggests that beliefs must be selectively mobilized to make sense of irrevocable action and the circumstances in which it was generated, even if all of this was only vaguely clear when the action itself became irrevocable (ibid.: 156). He points out how the question of volition rapidly becomes salient in this process. Were the actions clearly chosen? If so, the person is responsible, and acceptable justification becomes more urgent. Justification is often the result of focused attention by those involved that reveals new properties of a situation that unfocused attention missed.

Just as Schein focuses on his understanding of culture formation in small groups and the place of marker events in this process, to propose that cultural change at the 'macro level' of the organization involves leaders paying attention intentionally and directly influencing the meaning attached to significant or critical events in the life of the organization, so also Weick proposes a macro-level 'recipe' for building a setting that produces strong commitment (1995: 158): action, publicity, choice, high stakes and low tolerance of mistakes, all intensify strong and consistent social justification (although low tolerance of mistakes may, he argues, diminish choice). Such committed sense-making is not only rich in detail, he says, but also a source of order and value as it imposes a form of logic on the interpretation of action. Organizations that routinely create a context that is high in visibility, volition and irrevocability should generate stronger commitments and richer justifications, and should make more sense to members. An organization which creates contexts low in these dimensions will have fewer commitments, fewer reasoned justifications and more alternative possibilities concerning what subsequent action may mean and what interpretations it may validate. Such an organization will have a poorly defined sense of what it is and what it can do. Taken to extremes, such an organization is a non-organization: it neither takes binding actions nor makes compelling reasons.

It is interesting to see how these ideas support the organizational practice of increasingly elaborate performance contracts linking people throughout the organization in a network of mutual commitment to stretch targets, the actions they propose to take to achieve these and the milestones that will be seen along the way. I have noticed that the larger, more dispersed and more complex the organizations formed by mergers and acquisitions on an international scale, the more such formalized, public mutual promises of endeavour and the consequences of such endeavour become the favoured way to create strong organizational identity. Much organizational discourse involves both the articulation of these commitments and the justification of actions when called on to account for them in the light of what happens. Weick's perspective supports this activity, as he suggests that strong commitments encourage forceful, sustained action that can change demands, rather than adapt to them. Thus, reaffirming commitments and strengthening actions enables organizations to manipulate their environments (ibid.: 161).

> Commitment focuses the social construction of reality on those actions that are high in choice, visibility and irrevocability. The meaning of the actions becomes whatever justifications become attached to those actions, becoming stronger when subsequent events confirm them, generalize them to other issues, and persuade people to use them as premises in their own decisions. As these events unfold an increasing number of people become organized by an increasingly more explicit, more valid and more compelling ideology. Their joint activities make sense.
>
> (ibid.: 162)

Amid the complexity, equivocality and ambiguity created by the multiplicity of intentions, actions and interpretations in play in organizational life, managers who are searching for forms of control may find solace in the work of writers like Schein and Weick. They may aspire to act intentionally on the meaning-making processes at work in organizations to help them shape cultures, create conditions which will foster strong organizational identities and influence their environments in directional ways. They aspire to act on interlocking self-fulfilling prophecies, retrospective sense-making, and tightly coupled mutual expectations to create narratives which emphasize efficient, insightful strategic decision-making towards intended outcomes. Sense-making may be recruited in the service of confident, ambitious ideologies which are more likely to create the environments they expect and so can deal with. The discourse of successful business, the rhetoric of CEOs and the eulogies of change management 'best practice' is ripe with such views.

The experience of spontaneity and 'working live'

I would like to return now to my earlier story to notice other aspects and draw out other implications. First, I want to notice the very great sensitivity people have to the experience of spontaneity. We sense immediately whether others or we ourselves are being more or less spontaneous in our responses. Spontaneity is a quality of interaction which does not imply impulsiveness, thoughtlessness, lack of intention or lack of anticipation. The issue is not whether spontaneous action involves being conscious or unconscious of motivations and intentions. The issue is, I would argue, to do with the quality of self-consciousness experienced. I will explore what I mean by this. When Steve and George embarked on their opening attempt to influence the way projects were being organized, they began with clear ideas of what they were doing and why, and had ideas about what this might achieve. Steve launched into his plan spontaneously as he found himself choosing a moment to begin, a moment he recognized as the chatter of the gathering group was dying away. He 'risked' an opening gambit, in the same way that anyone speaking into the unknown is risking. However, as he and George continued, not exactly according to a script, but according to already outdated notions of what should happen next, rather than what was actually beginning to happen next, they became less and less 'present' and so increasingly unconvincing not just to others but, in a way they themselves acknowledged later, to themselves. They were playing themselves in an anticipated situation rather than finding themselves in the emerging situation. They sounded 'odd' in this sense, that they were sustaining ideas of themselves as characters in a scene which was diverging from the possible scenes that were developing in the responses being variously evoked around them. All this was beginning to happen even before those responses became verbal. Instead of improvising in response, which by no means implies abandoning their intention to influence how the projects might be organized, they continued responding to one another according to plan; they were no longer 'live'. They lost spontaneity, and it is interesting to see how as this was sensed, questions of trust, credibility, sincerity, authenticity, ethics and power-relating became explicitly examined and negotiated, not just in relation to Steve and George but in relation to everyone participating. These issues were then worked 'live', contributing to shifts in the webs of relations in the group, shifting the patterning of interaction.

I am not trying to hold up spontaneity as an ideal or prescription, rather to point out that the experience of feeling more or less spontaneous, more or less 'at risk', being more or less 'present' as a participant in evolving situations is crucial in human communicative action. We are sensitive to this in our own bodies and alert to this in other bodies. Any attempt to influence sense-making processes is exposed to these sharp sensors as we go about persuading one another about the real, the true, the worthwhile, the legitimate.

Mead's (1934) theories of the emergence of self-consciousness in the iteration of gesture/response in communicative activity provide more detailed insight. He suggests that the meaning of all communication between social creatures emerges in the iterations of gesture and response. The meaning of any social act requires both gesture and response, and because responses are being evoked even as the gesture is under way, gesture and response, and thus the meaning of the social act, continue to emerge during the act. Mead suggests that where evolution has favoured increasingly sensitive nervous systems capable of evoking in the gesturer bodily responses similar to those evoked in another towards whom one is gesturing, anticipation and consciousness become possible. Further, human beings have become capable of taking the attitude not just of particular others, but of their social group towards themselves, thus generating self-consciousness and the possibility of feelings of embarrassment, shame, pride and so on, all evoked spontaneously. 'In taking the attitude' of what he called the generalized other, Mead does not use the term 'attitude' as in opinion; rather, he is referring to *tendencies* of large numbers of one's society or culture to respond in certain ways in certain situations. Thus, as we are engaged in a public conversation of gesture and response with other human bodies, we are simultaneously engaged in a silent conversation of gesture and response experienced in our own bodies, and the meaning of what we are doing together is continuously emerging. In the public conversation the patterning of society is emerging; in the silent conversation the patterning of uniquely experienced selves is emerging and the two are inextricably mutually constitutive. Mead called the silent conversation of self the 'I–me dialectic', in which the sense of 'me' (the organized attitude of one's group/society) evoked by one's own actual and imagined actions in response to the actual and imagined gestures of others evokes a response from an 'I' which evokes a response of 'me' and so on. There is no separate 'I' and 'me'; rather, Mead says that they are different phases of the self process; it is this dialectic which creates our experience of being self-conscious persons. Mead draws attention to the fact that the response of the 'I' to the 'me' is always capable of spontaneity, thus potentially changing the individual and so of necessity contributing to change in society.

So in my story above, as Steve and George begin speaking in response to earlier gestures in both their silent and their public conversations, the process of evoking for each the organized attitudes of their respective social groups (largely similar but never entirely identical, because of their different histories of interaction) continues. Sensing some constraint in the hearing of others, the conventionalized me is answered by an 'I', which in this case means that they both plough ahead in the face of this sensed constraint. Mead's 'I–me' dialectic helps us understand how we can sound strange to ourselves. Then another person spontaneously expresses his view that 'You have rehearsed this', despite the conventionalized way in which we often do not interrupt one another in such a setting. Intended or not, this has a slightly accusatory note as it is spoken and heard. For a number of people, their own sensations listening to Steve and George are suddenly organized into possible meaning and they respond variously, and soon an entire conversation of significance for the life of this community of people is under way. The movement of sense-making is happening spontaneously and people are feeling the heightened sense of 'risk' as the patterning of personal and social identities is at work. In the way we are using the term in this book, this is ensemble improvisation; this is 'working live'.

I think it is important to draw attention to what the experience of this is actually like. It is one thing to advocate the management of the processes of meaning-making, as do Schein and Weick, and quite another to participate in these processes. In talking about managing the process, the spontaneous nature of the changes is either underplayed or misunderstood. The succeeding chapters of this volume will elaborate further what is involved in the experience of attempting to influence the meaning-making processes through which we organize.

The emergence of legitimizing explanations

Finally, having introduced some of the themes this volume is concerned with, I will tell another story of organizational change. I will tell it so as to draw attention to the way orienting ideas and concepts, legitimizing explanations and models, forms of mutual accounting and recognition, emerge 'live'. The scene is one afternoon of a two-day meeting of some forty managers from a manufacturing company seeking to expand its export activities. There has recently been a reorganization, retaining manufacturing sites in the original country but opening new sales, distribution and warehousing facilities in other continents. I have joined the group along with members of the Dacapo company to assist the managers make sense of the changes they are experiencing, and we are working with a form of play-back theatre: the managers have been asked to discuss the kinds of challenges they are facing, not in generalized terms but particularized in actual situations. As is sometimes the case, people struggle a little with this. Organizations tend to promote abstract models and frameworks for presenting what has occurred and for advocating courses of action. As I listen to the questions, which indicate some confusion and reluctance, I rise to sketch a framework for making sense of abandoning the more familiar form of exchange. My ideas are incomplete as I begin but are completed because by beginning I draw some responses, and as I hear myself speaking I also respond to both others and to myself. The framework that ends up on the wall is at once an individual and a social achievement. It makes sense of our situation and how we all may continue; it succeeds exactly because it is not pre-rehearsed but emerges 'live'.

Something similar occurred earlier when one of the company directors, joining the meeting in the morning to offer a 'strategic perspective', agreed not to give his prepared speech from the front, but rather to make his points as part of a live interview with Henry from Dacapo. Although prepared, he now improvised an exchange with Henry, with all the attendant increase in spontaneity, risk and increased interest from those listening. Whereas in delivering a prepared speech he could be less sensitive to audience response, in the live interview he and Henry and all those listening were participating in processes not unlike those I described in my earlier story, although much less overtly. What were being negotiated non-verbally through subtle shifts of tone, language, stance, expression, speed, pauses, experiences of tension mounting and releasing at different points, laughter and so on, were similar issues of credibility, plausibility, trust, confidence, authority and conviction. The sense of satisfaction created by this activity was again an individual and a social achievement. Although this would have been true also during a monologue from the stage, the potential for mutual responsiveness would be much reduced.

Going back to the framework, what goes up on the wall is a figure of eight. At the top is the phrase 'concepts and frameworks', at the bottom is the phrase 'scenes of everyday life' and at the centre of the crossing lines is the phrase 'connecting narratives'. This picture is created as a conversation develops about how the way people talk in organizations creates an unfortunate blind spot in which people are often unable to make the links between the detailed scenes of everyday life in which they participate, the narrative sense-making which creates and weaves those scenes, and the more generalized and abstract accounts of strategic direction that are becoming legitimized in their organizations. We explain how we can try working with improvisational theatre and ideas about emergence in social interaction to develop our appreciation of how those links are forged, and in so doing bring a new intelligibility to the challenges of managing and changing organizational practices.

Having made sense together of what we are up to, one manager offers to explore his experience of successfully negotiating a new contract in China. He explains that he is particularly interested in how nothing went according to the rule book. Henry Larsen asks him for a key scene from his story: what was happening, who was there and so on. The manager begins a number of possible scenes but interrupts himself with repeated 'no wait, we need to go back to . . .', or 'actually we need to begin with . . .', until, laughing, he settles for a scene on the aircraft on his way to China for a meeting with government officials. He and his colleague are settling into their seats prior to take-off. Having given some details of what happened, the Dacapo actors improvise a scene as the two managers interact with a Chinese businessman sitting in the front row. It is clear that the issue is what makes the difference between these three maintaining their relative identities as chance fellow passengers who remain strangers to one another, or risking allowing connection and relationship to develop, thereby changing their respective sense of moral sensibility and possibility in relation to one another. The scene stimulates discussion of this experience in a number of situations – what is it that enables openings between people and how does this create change? As people improvise the scenes in different ways there are vivid moments when ritualized exchanges turn on a spontaneous and unexpected response, and new directions develop.

It was because of this that the two managers were offered the opportunity of meeting their Chinese acquaintance's boss, who was the procurement manager of a large company in Shanghai. That led to further improvisation: they were not equipped to provide their company's selling pitch – they did not have appropriate materials and were not fully up to speed on what kind of deal would be most advantageous. Should they pass the contact to others or take up the opportunity based on a personal connection? This led to further improvisations about communication with sales colleagues back home and later meetings with supply departments when what was negotiated in China failed to match preferred procedures of the company. These scenes were set up and explored by the Dacapo actors and several managers at the meeting, who took up the improvisation to act into their interpretation of the developing situations. In the process the links we had talked about earlier between 'everyday life' and the strategies, policies and practices of the organization designed to support increased export activity came under scrutiny.

The head of the region whose managers were together at this meeting was so provoked by what the work was showing that he risked another spontaneous move. He suggested that the meeting opened up the discussion about the way the regional organization was working and the current proposals for further changes. The scenes of the last couple of hours had made him doubt that the thinking was as well developed as he now felt was needed. It was interesting that this move, experienced as surprising to many, generated a prolonged conversation in which important issues similar to those raised in my first story were negotiated. Was this a genuine move? What exactly did opportunistic mean? What were the ethics of opportunism? Was the executive risking his credibility? Was this undermining the project team who were working on these questions? A similar atmosphere of liveliness, interest and tension developed in which conflicts of interest, shifting alliances and power relations reorganized themselves live. The afternoon was later deemed memorable by many present, and significant in the evolution of the company's culture and strategy.

My intention in this first chapter was to introduce the key themes of this volume, the nature of spontaneous change in the sense-making processes through which we organize ourselves and the experiences of being more or less spontaneous, more or less at risk that are called forth in this process. In the following chapters the issues are taken up by others researching these questions through their experience as a consultant, actor and theatre director, senior manager and therapist. Finally, Ralph Stacey summarizes how the way of thinking we have called complex responsive processes of relating in organizations approaches these themes.

References

Kiesler, C. A. (1971) *The Psychology of Commitment*, New York: Academic Press.

Mead, G. H. (1934) *Mind Self and Society*, Chicago, IL: University of Chicago Press.

Schein, E. H. (1985) *Organizational Culture and Leadership*, San Francisco: Jossey-Bass.

Shaw, P. (2002) *Changing Conversations in Organizations: A complexity approach to change*, London: Routledge.

Weick, K. E. (1995) *Sensemaking in Organizations*, Thousand Oaks, CA: Sage.

Editors' introduction to Chapter 2

In this chapter, Preben Friis and Henry Larsen, both members of the Dacapo Theatre, present their thinking about the way in which they use improvisational theatre to consult to organizations. They understand the contribution this form of consulting makes to organizations in terms of a particular perspective on human communication taken from the work of George Herbert Mead. The essence of his thinking is that communication takes the form of gestures made by one person evoking responses from others and that it is in this temporal, relational process that meaning emerges. Meaning never lies in the gesture alone, but in the gesture taken together with the responses, so that the response has the potential for informing the gesture with new meaning. This is in fact an improvisational view of human communication. It follows that improvisation is not a skill located in an autonomous individual but, rather, a relational and spontaneously responsive activity. The approach Friis and Larsen take to their work, therefore, is one in which they deliberately foster spontaneous interaction between everyone involved in the work, including themselves. In doing this, they are not following a planned script; rather, they are improvising their way forward in the same way as the other participants while continuing to find out what emerges between them. What they are trying to do is to bring themselves and others into situations where no one can rely on carefully planned actions, but must risk responding spontaneously to one another. They argue that it is in this way that people are able to recognize themselves, each other and their work in new ways. They provide narratives of their work and argue that it is in ordinary improvisational, conversational activity that modes of practice and the abilities of practitioners come alive and evolve.

The authors compare their approach to improvisational theatre consulting with the work of other organizational writers who focus attention on improvisation. The views of most other authors in the field are based on a very different model of human communication which can be called the sender–receiver model. According to this model, ideas arise autonomously in individual minds, are coded in language and then transmitted to another, who decodes the signal so that the idea from the first mind then arises in the second mind. Meaning then lies in the word, and communication is thought of as an intentional act by an individual, which loses the notion of evoking responses and emergent meaning, and sees improvisation as something that primarily goes on in the individual. Friis and Larsen explore the consequences of sender–receiver perspectives on organizations. They argue that these lead to the reification of temporal process so that improvisation is turned into a tool that managers and consultants can apply to achieve the results they decide upon in advance. The authors of this chapter argue that in taking this view, the importance of relating between people and the spontaneity of that relating are downplayed. For Friis and Larsen, approaches based on the sender–receiver model do not explain the transformational processes that are so evident in theatre improvisation and everyday ordinary conversation.

2 Theatre, improvisation and social change

Preben Friis and Henry Larsen

- Involving the audience
- Reflections on our way of working
- Keith Johnstone and his way of understanding theatre improvisation
- Other ways of understanding improvisation in theatre work
- Relating organizational improvisation to theatre improvisation

The Dacapo Theatre consists of management consultants and theatre people plus a small administrative staff. In the summer of 2004 there were sixteen people working full time with organizational clients from the public and private sectors. Dacapo started some fifteen years ago with one actress and one internal consultant in a can factory in Denmark. Although they were not aware of it, they were part of a movement using theatre in organizations in a number of different countries. The work at the can factory developed slowly and after five years the two founders left the factory to form a professional, independent company. Today, Dacapo is well known in Denmark for its capacity to engage small and large audiences in a live dialogue about change processes taking place in organizations. At first, the method of working was mainly based on the Forum Theatre techniques developed by Augusto Boal ([1979] 2000, 1992, 1995). Forum Theatre is an interactive form of theatre where the audience is involved in trying to find solutions to problems raised in the play. Apart from performing a scripted play, this demands a high degree of improvising from the actors. The Dacapo consultant then facilitates this process between the audience and the actors. Dacapo has, however, developed these methods over a number of years. Where Boal talks about people as oppressors and oppressed, we talk about different people in an organization having different perspectives. Where Boal looks for solutions to problems, we are more concerned with how everyone in an organization may engage themselves in an evolving and continuous change process. The work of Dacapo used to take an event format, where we spent only one day with the same group of people in a company. It is now slowly turning towards being involved at different levels in the organization, with different issues and on a longer-term basis.

Accounting for the relevance of using theatre and improvisation in consultancy easily leads to seeing theatre and improvisation as methods or tools for creating certain results when used in client organizations. This is a cause–effect way of accounting for what is happening, which suggests that we are applying something from theatre to the organization. Our main interest is not primarily in exploring theatre as a tool, method or technique to be applied to organizations. Instead, we have come to focus on *improvisation and spontaneity* as communicative activities in *ordinary conversation.* In this chapter we explore the different ways in which improvisation is understood in the organizational literature, and we take as examples the work of Schein (1999), Kanter (2002) and Weick (1995, 2001, 2002). We focus on the nature of improvisation as we understand it and reflect on how these authors tend to draw different conclusions to ours. We think that these authors understand communication in terms of a sender–receiver model. In this model, messages are sent from one autonomous individual to another. The sender transmits a signal, which has a clear meaning in itself already formed in the mind of the sender. If the receiver cannot understand it, this is because the sender is not communicating clearly enough or because the receiver suffers from some kind of filter block. Here, communication is solely a tool for conveying messages, quite separate from sense-making and action. Processes of sense-making and creation of novelty take place within the individual. We have found this model of communication to be widely prevalent in most organizational thinking.

We have increasingly felt dissatisfied with communication understood in these terms. Within this framework, we find it difficult to explain and understand the nature of our work with theatre improvisation in organizations, and, in a broader sense, we find it difficult to understand what is going on in organizations if we take the sender–receiver perspective. Instead, we are drawn to other ways of understanding communication in terms of the relational activities of people. We are particularly attracted by the thinking of complex responsive processes of relating (Stacey *et al.*, 2000), which builds on the work of George Herbert

Mead (1934) and Norbert Elias ([1939] 2000). We are also inspired by our understanding of Keith Johnstone's (1981, 1997, 1999) work on theatre improvisation. We want to begin our exploration of the use of theatre improvisation in organizational consulting with an example of our work.

Involving the audience

> *Henry:* Dinga-linga-ling. . . . The phone is ringing in your OHS office – is anybody going to answer it?

We are working with fourteen people who have recently been hired by different Danish occupational health services (OHSs). They are working in different sectors all over Denmark and are now on a four-day introductory course. This is the third day, and the focus of the day is 'the role of the OHS consultant'. OHS is a consultancy directed towards health and safety in private and public organizations, work that has to be understood in broad terms. Most of these fourteen participants are psychologists, one or two are ergonomics specialists and physiotherapists, and one is an engineer. It is 9 a.m. and we are going to work with them until 5.30 p.m.

> *Henry:* Dinga-linga-ling . . .

We have split them into three groups each forming an OHS consultancy. We have told them that Preben will act as different persons from a company who will contact the OHS for help. They have just talked for ten minutes about their understanding of what being a consultant in an OHS means.

> *Henry:* Dinga-linga-ling . . . Is nobody going to answer the phone?

Eventually someone (A) improvises picking up the phone.

> *A:* OHS Jutland, can I help you?
> *Preben/* My name is Christian Hansen. I'm calling from KM
> *Christian:* Productions where I am managing the canteen. We have a small problem and I wonder if you could help us? We are using chlorine in the dishwasher, but we would really like to find an alternative.
> *A:* Why are you using chlorine?
> *Pre/Chr:* The dishes are not clean if we don't.
> *A:* Have you always used chlorine in the dishwasher?

Pre/Chr: No, we stopped when we became ecological. But after some time we had complaints that the dishes weren't clean and so we began using chlorine again. But I think you can understand that being an ecological canteen yet using chlorine is not really appropriate.

The dialogue continues like this for a while, and A promises to see if he can find an alternative to the chlorine. The conversation ends. Henry asks the three consultancies to talk about what happened in the conversation. They do this for five minutes and come back with comments like: 'He shouldn't have promised to find an alternative, that's not our job.' 'He should have asked more questions – maybe it's the machine.' 'He should have asked for a meeting.'

They have many suggestions about what he should have done instead of what he did. We are not surprised by this response because we encounter it all the time and it reflects a widespread view of how we learn. According to this view, we learn by talking about the mistakes we make and about how to correct them the next time we find ourselves in the same situation. Some years ago we shared this view and replayed the scene, going back in time to repeat the same telephone call to see how the ideas that had come up in discussion would change the conversation. We no longer do this, not so much because it is unrealistic, but rather because it gives the impression that there is a right way to handle such a conversation and if we can find the right way, or at least a better way, we will be able to improve next time. Of course we do learn from reflecting on our mistakes, but not in such a mechanistic way. The suggestions people have about what A should have done differently are formed on the basis of what happened in that particular conversation with the benefit of hindsight. But we live our lives forwards despite understanding them backwards. We understand what we should have done then, but if we now repeat it, it will be different in some way. A different question or suggestion will lead to a different response from Christian and so they will once again find themselves in a situation that was not planned. Training the consultants in this first contact with a client by repeating the conversation many times and reflecting on it would improve their skills, of course, but the first conversation can lead to a large number of different next steps and each of these can again lead to a large number of next steps. It would be impossible to train the consultants to meet all of these situations. Whatever we do, the consultants will repeatedly find themselves in situations that were not planned and could have been handled better with the benefit of hindsight. Our session on this day is not about training the consultants in opening conversations but about consulting as a form of improvisation. That is why we do not repeat the conversation. Instead, the dialogue proceeds as follows:

Henry: Now that you know what you've been talking about and you know what happened in the telephone conversation with Christian – what will you do next? – Talk about that for a few minutes in your group.

They talk and Henry asks who has a suggestion.

B: I would like to know more about the machine, I think there's something wrong with the machine. So I would phone Christian back and . . .

As soon as Henry hears an idea about how to proceed, he interrupts by saying:

Henry: Dinga-linga-ling . . .
Pre/Chr: Christian Hansen, canteen.
B: Eh . . . I'm B from OHS Jutland.
Pre/Chr: Yes, hi . . . (Leaving it open to B to decide whether he is the same character as A phoning back or a colleague.)
B: I would like to ask a couple more questions. Is the machine OK?
Pre/Chr: It's a very good dishwasher and it's just been serviced a couple of weeks ago. Did you find an alternative fluid?
B: Eh . . . (His strategy has already collapsed). No, not yet. . . . Would it be OK if I visited you and looked at the machine?
Pre/Chr: No problem, you're welcome any time, but what I need really is a new fluid for the dishwasher so I would appreciate it if you would look into that.

B promises to do that and they agree on a date for the visit. End of phone call.

Henry: OK, B – now it's the agreed date and here is Christian meeting you in the canteen.
Pre/Chr: Hi! Welcome. Did you solve our little problem with the chlorine?
B: Eh . . . we're working on it.

B feels pressured now. He had a theory and a strategy about the problem when he answered the phone. Both collapsed after ten seconds and instead he grasps at another idea, which has been mentioned, to visit the canteen kitchen. Henry sets up the meeting directly and throws him into the new situation because the focus of the day is to explore with them a different way of thinking about consulting: improvised consulting. As the day evolves we realize that most of the consultants understand consulting in terms of the following steps:

1 Gather information.
2 Analyse the situation.
3 Make a plan that will solve the problems.
4 Agree the plan with the client.
5 Implement the plan.

As the work continues, the consultants realize that the chlorine is just a minor problem. They have met Alice, who has worked in the kitchen for some years and who is enthusiastic about the new way of working where the employees now take most of the daily decisions. It has meant a tremendous rise in quality, she says, which again has meant more customers, which again means working faster and longer hours, and means they have had to speed up the dishwasher, which means the plates aren't clean and so they have gone back to using chlorine. That's her story about the chlorine. So yes, there are minor problems, but nothing compared to the excitement of being part of a team which is succeeding in creating a high-quality ecological canteen.

They have talked to the health and safety representative, who is angry because the employees are breaking the safety regulations, but the manager and the rest of the employees are unwilling to do anything about it. The consultants also met Anna-Maria, who has problems with the new way of working and who would rather make meatballs as she has always done. She has had a nervous breakdown and just come back to work. She is a very timid person who will not complain about anything. Christian, the canteen manager, has shown the consultants that he is aware that they are breaking some of the health and safety regulations and that Anna-Maria is under pressure from the other employees, who are working very hard and sometimes extra hours without pay. But it is their own decision and it is really for the benefit of everybody, because in six months the canteen will no longer receive money from the company of which it is a part, and if it cannot support itself it will be closed.

This is the complex picture the OHS consultants have become aware of after a few hours.

Henry asks them what they, as consultants, are going to do about it. Some suggest that they just solve the chlorine problem, which is what they have been asked to do in the first place, but most feel that they should address some of the serious underlying problems and involve themselves in the messy situation of the canteen.

It may appear that we are conducting this training session by following a planned script, but in fact we are improvising our way forward just like the participants. We have worked with the staff of the canteen on other occasions, and so we have a picture of some of the characters, such as Christian, the canteen manager, Alice and Anna-Maria. However, in each situation with the consultants on stage, the actor has to take on whatever character is needed and improvise. Although we have an idea of the organization, it also emerges for us as we are working. The focus of the actor is to create realistic situations and to play the characters in a way which will challenge the consultants. This means the consultants will often be surprised at what happens, but so will the actor. It is also the task of the actor to create a complex picture of an organization, one in which there is no 'truth', but all characters have their own perspective of what has happened and is happening, and why. So, of course, we have intentions about how we would like to challenge the consultant and we are constantly influencing what is happening. But we are also not in control of what is happening because we must respond to the intentions of our fellow player coming on stage. On this occasion the actor had to play several characters we have never seen before but had to invent on the spot in response to who the consultants wanted to meet.

The consultants discuss again what to do in their three little consultancies, and what happens is interesting. They are setting up one meeting after the other – with Christian, Alice, Anna-Maria and others – but always with just one person. What they are trying to do is obviously to gather enough information to be able to analyse the situation in order to come up with a plan which will solve the problems. They have had ideas about how to start handling some of the problems. They have made agreements with one person in one meeting only to find in the next meeting with another person that the plan does not work. So, they start once again gathering information to be able to come up with a better plan. After two hours we stop and talk about what is happening.

They are frustrated because they are getting nowhere. They have enough information to see that there is no obvious solution that will satisfy everyone. They have then tried to decide which problem is the most urgent and to start with that. But trying to solve one problem has amplified others and they find themselves going round in circles. This is where the participants divide, with two main opinions emerging. One group say that they must decide a plan and a strategy and start implementing it now, or leave. 'The problem is', one says, 'that our indecisiveness is making the situation worse. They are waiting for us to come up with something and if we don't they would be better off without us. Then they would at least know they had to deal with the problems themselves.' The other group are mainly frustrated because they have not been able to help. 'There is something basically wrong in our way of handling this situation,' one says. This leads to other questions: What if we cannot find a plan that will solve the situation? What if we can never know beforehand what will happen in the next moment? As we are talking, most of the people agree that this is the way it is. That is the experience of what we have been doing so far. But if this is the way it is, what then is consulting? This becomes the turning point for the rest of the day.

Reflections on our way of working

So how do we think about what we are doing when we work with organizations in this way? We are deliberately bringing people and ourselves into spontaneous activity where all of us must improvise our way forward while continuing to find out what emerges between us. The theme of the day is *the role of the consultant*. We could attempt to work with this as though it were separate from our lived experience, which could be discussed and learned about and then implemented in our working lives. However, we think that it is more fruitful to bring us all into situations where we cannot rely on our carefully planned actions, where we must risk responding spontaneously to one another, where we are able to recognize ourselves, each other and our work in new ways and so reflect differently on what we are doing. In this way, modes of practice and our abilities as practitioners come alive and evolve.

In the previous chapter Shaw points to how Schein (1999) stresses the predictable nature of an organization's development so that such development is in a sense already existing and we just need to be able to understand it. Schein talks about the need for the consultant to improvise, but this has a different meaning for him from the one it has for us. Let us explore what kinds of problems we see in Schein's way of thinking when it comes to our work with the consultants described above.

Schein uses the sender–receiver model of communication described earlier in this chapter, involving autonomous individuals each with their own filters of interpretation and independent intentions. Individual minds are understood to be separate systems and the organization is seen as a system too, all systems being separated from each other by boundaries. Such separation means that there needs to be some common ground if any communication is to take place, and so care is needed to ensure that 'the right message gets across', to which end some principles and guidelines for communications are given (1999: 133–140). He adds to this that 'each of us has a unique personal history that in effect creates a set of filters for how we communicate to others and how we hear and perceive them' (ibid.: 116). These filters, which we are not always conscious of, operate as defensive mechanisms and distort our observation and listening skills, making communication difficult. So, sense-making is going on in the individual, and communication is conveying messages about what is going on in each of these individual systems. Schein sees the process consultant as someone who is more trained to observe the effects of the filters. He therefore suggests that the main work of the process consultant is to help the client to diagnose and reflect on what is happening. Schein explains what goes on inside the mind of individuals in terms of a four-step process: observation; emotional reaction; judgement; and intervention. This is very close to the ideas that many of the consultants from the occupational health services had of consulting work. This provides a basis for conscious, rational decisions on what actions should be taken to reduce distortions and miscommunication and so change the culture of the organization.

For Schein, the primary focus for the consultant should be on 'process':

> Consultants/helpers must recognize that process, i.e. *how* things are said and done, is as or more important than content, i.e. *what* is said and done. Yet most of us are not very familiar with process as a concept or focus of attention.
>
> (1999: 145)

Schein understands this work as improvised. He writes, 'Helping is a performance art more akin to improvisational theatre than to formal drama' (ibid.: 107). However, improvisation for him means to 'learn . . . how to create the right scenes and to manage the dramatic process towards a desirable outcome' (ibid.: 108). Even though he talks about 'audience participation', he sees this as a stream of feedback signals to the consultants, who must therefore 'be prepared to rewrite their scripts constantly' (ibid.: 107). Rewriting the script continually, as Schein suggests, will mean focusing on what happens before and after the action itself, on planning, on reflecting, on feedback, all going on in the individual. Then one thinks that change happens as a result of deliberate actions on the basis of certain parameters which we choose to identify as causing the result. The emphasis is then on becoming more skilled in understanding and handling these chosen parameters. In the situation we have just described, this would mean that the consultants would need to analyse before they act. In our experience this makes it difficult to be present in the sense of actually participating in the ongoing emerging conversation, precisely in line with what the OHS consultants experienced.

Stacey draws attention to the implications of taking a systemic perspective on interaction:

> If one takes a systemic perspective . . . then interaction, participation
> and process have a very particular meaning. As parts of a system,
> individuals are interacting with each other to produce a system.
> Participation means that they participate as parts of the system that
> their interaction creates. The meaning of process within the system is
> that of interaction to produce a system. In all of these cases,
> interaction creates something that is abstracted from direct experience
> of interaction itself.
>
> (2003: 272)

We think that we need to bring attention to interaction among humans as such. In the ongoing improvisation described earlier, we all had to act spontaneously, *without being on top of our own action*, and this interaction in itself creates the next moments. In contrast to Schein's understanding of communication in terms of autonomous systems (individuals) sending messages to each other, and an understanding of improvisation as rewriting 'the' script, assuming that there is one, we think that meaning emerges for all of us in the ongoing improvised conversation (Mead, 1934). In conversation, gesturing cannot be separated from responding; it is seen as one act. Meaning emerges in this act as gesturing/responding, which again calls forth other responses that become gestures (see Chapter 6 in this volume for a fuller explanation). The OHS consultants created intentions in the midst of the work, some of them tried out their intentions, and as they did so, their intentions changed, as did the responses from us. We have gradually come to realize the radical difference Mead's view of communication makes. Communication is no longer a tool for sending messages, but the essence of becoming who we become, and creating what we create together. In the following section we will explore this assertion by drawing attention to the work of Keith Johnstone on theatre improvisation.

Keith Johnstone and his way of understanding theatre improvisation

Keith Johnstone (1981, 1997, 1999) has never worked in organizational theatre. Nevertheless, he has had a tremendous influence not only on the work of Dacapo, but also on most theatre work involving improvisation. He began developing his ideas and exercises in the late 1950s and started a theatre company called The Theatre Machine, which toured Europe with entirely improvised shows. Later he took up the teaching of improvisation in drama schools, theatre companies, teacher training colleges and many other places. His ideas are based on spontaneous improvisation and the notion that new creative ideas emerge and are developed in the relationship *between* players, not in the exceptional individual. Let us explore how he works by going into one of his exercises and our experience with it.

The bench

We are working with fifteen leaders and designers from the R & D department of a big toy company. 'We' are the Dacapo Theatre and today we are working with improvisation. This is one of the improvisation games run by Preben:

> I ask for two volunteers to sit on a bench. Then I tell them that they have to leave the bench for a specific reason and it has to be the same reason for both of them. They are not allowed to talk, but may communicate in any other way. And as soon as they think that they have found a mutual reason for leaving, they should get up and do so. 'You should have told us that before we got up here,' one of them said, 'I don't have any ideas.' 'Don't worry,' I said, 'just wait and see what happens.' After doing nothing for a while, one person gets an idea: he is looking at his watch and signals that he has to hurry. The other one is not reacting, but shortly afterwards he offers another idea: he starts shivering as though he is feeling cold and looks to his companion, but is getting no reaction. They continue like this for a while, blocking each other's ideas. The audience is getting bored. I stop and ask why they have not left. They say they thought the ideas were not good enough. I tell them the idea is good if it helps them to

leave the bench. The only important criterion is that they both agree why they are leaving. They start again and soon one is putting a hand out and looks at the sky. The other one does the same. They look at each other – they agree it's raining. They nod their heads, get up and rush off. The audience is pleased.

Now I ask the two on the bench to go one step further. They still have to leave the bench for the same reason, but neither of them is allowed to decide autonomously on the idea as to why they are leaving. The idea has to emerge in the situation, and no one should afterwards be able to tell where the idea came from. They do not believe that it is possible; an idea has to come from somewhere. But they try and they fail, because they cannot bear to just sit there waiting to see what happens. So after a while one of them starts killing mosquitoes, the other one picks them up, and soon they leave. I ask the audience who had the idea, and they are in no doubt. Two more people try and then quite a few more. But the audience can always tell who initiated the idea.

The group is frustrated, so we leave the exercise and do something else for a few hours, and then we return to it. In the meantime we have been laughing a lot and the atmosphere is quite relaxed. Two more people go to the bench. They sit down and wait. They look at each other, they are very attentive, they have good eye contact and cannot help smiling. Suddenly they are flirting and they leave. The audience concludes that they left because they wanted to go home and make love, and the actors agree. I ask who conceived the idea. Some in the audience say it was neither of them, others that it was both at the same time, others that it just happened.

From many exercises, we have chosen this one because it focuses on novelty as emerging between the actors. We are aware that we create a very specific and rather odd situation, but we think that it focuses on what we find to be important about improvisation.

The nature of improvisation

How can we make sense of an exercise like this, and why do we find it important? In the actors' struggle to find a reason for leaving the bench, the action is about recognizing each other. The movement towards this cannot be done without people relating to each other and, in doing this, also to some extent recognizing each other. In the particular case with the couple creating a romance this process of recognition happened as an iteration of responses to each other's gestures. One makes a tiny move on the bench, one that he or she might not even notice. Sitting on a bench being watched by an audience makes it impossible to 'just sit'. One becomes a bit uneasy, and starts to do something, not being master of one's own actions. So, the tiny movement is not made with clear and express intention, but if it is noticed by the other there will follow a reaction. In these iterations of re-action, intention emerges and becomes stronger between them. When you sit on the bench you are fully aware that people in the audience are watching you, and it might feel safer not to relate to the other at certain moments, but, obviously, without relating you will never find a reason to leave the bench. Also, it feels much safer to let one person take the initiative, but for the audience this is boring to watch, because it is easy to see that nothing new is emerging. However, to those sitting in the audience it is very interesting to follow the struggle of the actors to create meaning together, to follow the work of finding a reason to leave the bench together. Leaving because a romance is emerging seems obvious, but again, when you sit on the bench it is risky to follow that emerging intention, because you might feel ridiculed in front of the other and in front of the audience if you misinterpret something. So, in the middle of the work there is a feeling of not being safe, that what is going on is somehow risky. This exercise makes it possible to experience change as something you cannot be in control of, although at the same time you have to participate to make it possible. What you can control is not to prevent something from happening. Streatfield (2001) says something similar when he notices that in organizations managers have to live with the paradox of being in control and not being in control at the same time.

Improvisational actors have to be able to change on stage by re-acting towards the other's action. This happens not for just a single actor, but for all of them at the same time, which is what creates the new scene. Johnstone talks about the importance of the actor accepting the offer made by the other actors. This is not just about listening, but about allowing yourself to react differently to what you hear, to allow yourself to change. This is not easy for actors, but it is what the audience is waiting for and enjoys when it happens.

There is a difference between actors improvising on stage, doing exercises like 'the bench', and real life, because in real life we know much more about each other – and there is no audience watching you as 'the actor'. That said, there are also huge similarities, because even if we anticipate the other's reaction we cannot know for sure what it will be, and if we try to control it nothing new can happen. Also, in real life, even if there is no formal audience, there is always somebody watching what is going on and you imagine what they think about it. And in real life it is not easy to allow yourself to change in your attitude towards yourself and others.

If we understand communication as the sending of messages to each other we cannot explain the events of the bench exercise. One person on the bench has to conceive of the idea and convey the message to the other. Change then goes on as a kind of black box inside the individual. However, in the way Mead talks about communication the events on the bench are understandable. Mead says that the response informs the gesture in a relational process. 'The meaning of a gesture by one organism is found in the response of another organism to what would be the completion of the act of the first organism which that gesture initiates and indicates' (1934: 146). This is what happened in the exercise with the bench. By constantly completing each other's gestures the two find a reason for leaving the bench. At the same time their own intention emerges and changes.

Obviously, we can only act in the present moment. However, the response informs the previous gesture with new meaning. This is the situation in the bench, but it is also the situation for the consultants at the beginning of this chapter. Also, for the individual consultant who partly consciously and partly unconsciously made a gesture, the perceptions of the past and the future at this very moment influence the actual conversation, but the present conversation also influences their perception of the past and their intentions for the future in relating to the client. In the midst of this the consultant has to improvise, in a sense that is very different from the understanding Schein is talking about when he articulates this as 'rewriting the script', because it goes on in the present moment. Mead developed this way of understanding the notion of 'present':

> Given an emergent event, its relations to antecedent processes become conditions or causes. Such a situation is a present. It marks out and in a sense selects what has made its peculiarity possible. It creates with its uniqueness a past and a future. As soon as we view it, it becomes a history and a prophecy. Its own temporal diameter varies with the extent of the event.
>
> ([1932] 2002: 52)

Mead is saying that the present moment can be marked out because of its peculiarity, because it momentarily creates a past and a future. This has implications for how we may think about consulting. Instead of pausing in the present to try to learn from the past to better design the future, as Schein suggests, we may think of what we are doing as continuously constructing the future together by making sense in the present. What we as consultants are involved in, then, is a paradoxical process of constructing a future that is constructing us at the same time. According to Shaw, this means that 'the potential for both stability and change is arising between us as the constraints of history are reshaped spontaneously, changing the meaning of the past and the future in the immediate experience of relating' (2002: 129). It is on this basis that we see our consultancy work. In this work, improvisation and spontaneity become very important, and ways of understanding the implications of this are explored in the next two chapters.

Other ways of understanding improvisation in theatre work

Many have taken up Johnstone's work to help business leaders improve their improvisation skills. However, most of them, especially in the United States, have taken the essence out of his work in order to streamline it for businesses. For example, Gesell (2005a) defines a goal for each exercise, while Carroll in relation to the consulting product 'Skills4success' (Carroll, 2005) says, 'We solve people's problems', and in this way they both reduce Johnstone's work to just another tool. Even though Keefe states that his consultancy product "Improv" is a discovery process' (2003: 111), he also says that 'Improv' is important to organizations because 'they can incorporate it as a tool before it is needed. By learning and applying Improv basics, organizations are supposed to be able to employ it when and where Improv is most valuable' (ibid.: 142). So, a process is reified and made into a tool. Addressing leaders, he says, 'If you aspire to great leadership, a basic understanding of improvisation is as important as courage. Read on leader; we'll get you there' (ibid.: 10). So, after all, he does see improvisation as a skill located in the individual. Also, Gesell understands the improvisational activity as going on in the individual, saying, 'In improv, players create reality through individual action and honest emotion while at the same time they develop a shared vision with other players' (2005b: 1).

Improvisation has become a frequently used term in organizational literature over the past fifteen years, and in 2002 an anthology was published (Kamoche *et al.*, 2002). In a review paper Cunha *et al.* (2002: 97) divided the research in this field into three stages. In the first stage, researchers explored activities where improvisation is standard practice, mainly jazz, to present a list of characteristics that can be transposed to organizational settings. In the second stage, empirical and anecdotal examples of improvisation in organizational settings were researched, to define the characteristics of improvisation in those settings. Third-stage researchers question the theories developed in the first two stages, which were grounded in analogies of improvisation in jazz with the aim of fine-tuning the understanding of the characteristics of organizational improvisation. Cunha *et al.* mention in their paper that 'improvisation seems to be an attractive concept for organizations, especially for those in the business area' (ibid.: 131), thereby taking a perspective of understanding improvisation as a deliberately chosen tool for someone in a company.

Most of the work on organizational improvisation has drawn on jazz improvisation as a key metaphor for organizational improvisation – for example, Hatch (2002), Barrett (2002), Bastien and Hostager (2002) and particularly Weick (2001, 2002), who has brought jazz as an analogy for organizational improvising into the mainstream. Others have also used theatre improvisation as metaphors or analogies for organizational improvisation (Kanter, 1977; Crossan and Sorrenti, 2002; Vera and Crossan, 2004). We will explore the thinking mainly of Weick, and also briefly the work of Kanter and Crossan, to notice similarities and differences from our thinking in the works of these authors.

Weick and jazz improvisation

In his earlier work, Weick (1995) explored sense-making in organizations, based on constructivist thinking. He acknowledged surprise, dissonance, failures and uncertainty as important in sense-making and he recognized these as creating situations where novelty can originate. Where Schein thinks in terms of a script before acting, Weick says that meaning for an organization is retrospective and the organization takes form when people make sense of the situation they find themselves in. In this way, sense-making becomes a relational process in which people co-create their environment and construct their identities. Weick's way of understanding sense-making is much closer to the way we understand the work we do in organizations, which is linked to the ideas of improvising. It is therefore interesting to look at possible differences.

Weick quotes the jazz musician Berliner in defining improvisation:

> I find it hard to improve the following definition, which is the one that guides this essay: 'Improvisation involves reworking precomposed material and designs in relation to unanticipated ideas conceived, shaped, and transformed under the special conditions of performance, thereby adding unique features to every creation'.
>
> (2001: 286)

In these terms, novelty seems to appear by *combining existing elements* in a new way. It is the special conditions of performance that adds novelty.

Weick refers to Stan Getz, who describes improvisation in terms of a language: 'you *learn* an *alphabet, which are the scales*, and you *learn* the *sentences which are the chords*, and you *then talk extemporaneously*' (ibid.: 293). Usually jazz improvisation is played in ensembles and with an audience, and therefore we argue that a kind of conversation is going on. However, here the focus is on the speaking, not on the conversing. Weick seems not to appreciate conversation as important for improvisation, novelty and transformation.

Weick also refers to another jazz musician, Max Roach:

> After you initiate the solo, one phrase determines what the next is going to be. From the first note you hear, you are responding to what you've just played: you just said this on your instrument, and now that's a constant. What follows from that? And then the next phrase is constant. What follows from that? And so on and so forth. And finally, let's wrap it up so that everybody understands that that's what you're doing. It's like language you are talking, you're speaking, you're responding to yourself. When I play, it's like having a conversation with myself.
>
> (ibid.: 291)

Here we see a focus on the present moment, on what has just happened, and what is next, about finding oneself in the middle of a flow in which one can conduct an internal conversation. However, Weick focuses on another element: he notices the importance of retrospect. What he notices is that form, memory and practice are all 'key determinants of success in improvisation'. To improve memory is to gain retrospective access to a greater range of resources, Weick says. In this we hear an understanding of the past as a fixed reality that you build upon when you improvise. This does not resonate with our experience. As the OHS consultants got involved with different people from the kitchen, their experiencing of the past changed and took on a new meaning for them. The present situation changed the perception of the past.

Weick concludes that the learning, absorption and use of certain underlying conventions in jazz allow the player to create a living work. If you are a bad and inexperienced trumpet player, you will be an even worse improviser of jazz music. Weick quotes Berliner as saying, 'Improvisation depends, in fact, on thinkers having absorbed a broad base of musical knowledge, including myriad conventions that contribute to formulating ideas logically, cogently, and expressively' (Weick, 2001: 286). To be a good jazz improviser you need to be skilled and experienced, and to know about musical structures. In addition, you must be able to use your experience and knowledge in an intuitive way. So, improvising means acting in two apparently opposite ways: being skilled and experienced in what you are dealing with; and at the same time acting into the unknown. Only if you are able to hold this paradox will you be a good improviser. However, it is important to say that improvising does not guarantee success. You may intuitively choose to do something which turns out to be a disaster in the particular situation. And improvising does not necessarily lead to novelty – it may also lead to repetition of old patterns. In understanding the use of experience in this process, the key word for Weick becomes *intuition*, and he tones down the importance of spontaneity. Weick says, 'intuition desperately needs to be unpacked, because it is the very nature of this process that makes improvisation possible and separates good from bad improvisation' (2001: 286). Weick draws on this way of thinking and relates it closely to his understanding of organizational improvisation.

Weick describes how jazz musicians take turns, each improvising in his or her own way on the musical theme. One may be influenced by the other but, basically, each musician challenges him- or herself in the improvisation. Weick, therefore, writes about jazz improvisation from an individual point of view. He says, 'The trick in improvisation is . . . to aim for clarity . . . on a not-too-obvious level' (2001: 290). This is the problem one faces in solo improvising: that of having to 'aim for clarity' but 'on a not-too-obvious level'. So, you have to aim for clarity, but at the same time you have to not aim for clarity because that would make the improvisation uninteresting. Weick is saying that the conflict or the dichotomy between clarity and not-clarity is important. There has to be a tension between the two and the single musician has to produce both. So, some musicians are skilled or gifted improvisers and others are not, which again may mean that if you want to use improvisation in your band you have to look for the right people – as Weick writes, 'Improvisation has implications for staffing' (ibid.: 299).

We do not find this way of thinking about improvising to be very helpful for organizations. We cannot imagine a manager who would 'aim for clarity . . . on a not-too-obvious level'. Managers aim for clarity but they may not all be aiming for the same clarity, or they may do it in different ways, or they may be surprised by something happening which makes the situation unclear and not-too-obvious. So, the tension between clarity and not-clarity will be there but not created in a single person. The tension will arise in the web of connections between everybody involved. This means that the improvisation is not in each individual but between the involved persons, where each of them is aiming for clarity. This implies that we understand improvising in organizations as going on in the interplay of people, not inside each individual.

To sum up:

● Weick focuses on intuition combined with knowledge of the past and underplays the importance of spontaneity in improvisation.
● We see this as linked to a way of understanding improvisation as something going on in the individual cognitive mind in contrast to our understanding of improvisation as spontaneity created between humans.
● Weick sees meaning as retrospective, which means we are making sense of our experience. We would rather say that making sense is an inseparable part of experiencing, where the past is changing its meaning in the light of the present and its expectations for the future.

Strategy as improvisational theatre

In trying to understand how innovation goes on in successful companies, Rosabeth Moss Kanter (2001, 2002) challenges the mainstream way of looking at innovation strategies as scripted plans. Scripted plans are like scripted theatre – slow and predictable. A scripted strategy resembles traditional theatre. The play is painstakingly written and rehearsed, and the actors practise their roles by repeating their words until they meet expectations for quality and predictability. Then they meet the audience, and the action comes to an unvarying conclusion in each performance. Pacesetter companies tend to act before they have a complete plan, she says, and she argues for taking the metaphor of theatre improvisation seriously, because it 'throws out the script, brings in the audience, and trusts the actors to be unpredictable – that is, to innovate' (Kanter, 2002: 76). She prefers the theatre improvisation metaphor to the jazz metaphor, because 'it shifts attention from the dynamics among the members of the project team to the way in which an organization as a whole can become an arena for staging experiments that can transform the overall strategy' (ibid.: 76).

Kanter operates with six elements around which strategic improvisation takes shape:

- *Themes.* Improvisation is chaos unless it is driven by a clear theme – a topic or headline that engages imagination and gets the action started.
- *Actors.* The actors must be willing to take unfamiliar roles, be attuned to each other and take cues from each other.
- *Theatres.* Innovators need a place to develop the play, a space of their own in which to rehearse and perform before they show their work to the audience.
- *Audience.* Business dramas have multiple audiences – customers, employees, investors, etc. – and members should be brought into the action as it unfolds.
- *Suspense.* A tolerance for suspense is required as no one, not even the actors, knows exactly how the drama will end. Everything can look like a failure in the middle.
- *Successive versions.* False starts and wrong moves are acceptable as long as audience feedback is rapid. Kanter argues that the slogan from total quality management – 'do it right the first time' – is not viable, because what is 'right' is not clear.

Kanter mentions that improvisation should be driven by a clear theme, but she does not talk about how this clear theme emerges and becomes a clear theme. She mentions that it might take the form of a leader's statement about a future destination, but she also mentions that 'improvisers must be willing to take action without having all the information they need' and 'at the pacesetter companies in my research, decisions affecting new ventures tended to be made by people with the most information rather than those with the highest status'. She argues for 'theatre' as a place to rehearse the improvisation, perhaps informally as 'skunkwork', but she does not go into the processes of improvisational innovation and the way it might be linked to improvisational theatre. Kanter mentions that 'effective improvisation requires dynamic visionaries whose belief is unwavering'. In this we hear an understanding of a singular individual who gets the idea and goes in front. Fonseca (2002) draws attention to how Kanter repeatedly focuses on the importance of exceptional individuals as the innovating character.

Her thinking does represent a challenge to the position of control and the idea of looking at the company and strategy from outside, since it obviously will not be possible to be in the same kind of control of the improvisational process. But the reference to improvisational theatre becomes a loose metaphor as she is not explaining how the novelty actually happens in the improvisation, whether in theatre improvisation or in organizational improvisation.

Relating organizational improvisation to theatre improvisation

Mary Crossan writes about working with theatre improvisation in organizations and has for years been working with the possible links between theatre improvisation and improvisation in organizations. She worked with Second City Theatre Company in Canada teaching improvisations to managers (Vera and Crossan, 2004: 731).

In 1997 she wrote 'Making Sense of Improvisation' with Marc Sorrenti (Crossan and Sorrenti, 2002) in an attempt to reflect on improvisation in organizations and how we can understand it. They defined improvisation in organizations as 'intuition guiding action in a spontaneous way'. There had been an academic discussion about this with Weick, who at that time preferred to focus on the importance of intuition and bricolage ('making things work by ingeniously using whatever is at hand') over spontaneity. Crossan and Sorrenti focused on spontaneity in daily improvisation by referring to Mintzberg, who observed that over 90 per cent of the verbal contacts of CEOs were not planned (1973: 36). They notice that often we tend to hesitate to answer quickly, but very often time is a scarce resource, and failing to respond may mean losing an opportunity (Crossan and Sorrenti, 2002: 30).

In 2004 Vera and Crossan raised the question 'What can organizations learn from theatrical improvisation?' (Vera and Crossan, 2004: 729). Here they contribute to a theory of improvisation by studying the principles and techniques that determine success in improvisational performances in theatre in order to shed light on the performance implications of improvisation in organizational settings (ibid.: 728). They find that the metaphor of theatre improvisation has several advantages over the jazz metaphor when it comes to accessibility, transferability and practice.

In order to understand jazz we need specialized musical knowledge, whereas theatre improvisation is based on speech, gestures and movement, which are materials in everyday action. The raw materials are words, not music.

Vera and Crossan notice other similarities between theatre and organizational improvisation. They find that improvisation is present in all drama, and the same applies to organizations. They see scripted and improvised work in theatre as a continuum. There is more scripted than improvised acting in a Shakespearian piece and more improvisation than script in a sequence of improvisational theatre games. They find a similar full spectrum in organizations, from adjustment to standard procedures at the one end to radical examples of improvisation in firms dealing with crisis events. In organizations they then define improvisation as 'the spontaneous and creative process of attempting to achieve an object in a new way' (ibid.: 733). Also, here there seems to be a link to the way they understand theatre improvisation. They refer to Viola Spolin: 'setting out to solve a problem with no preconception as to how you will do it' (ibid.: 731). In both quotations there seems to be a defined object to achieve, or problem to solve.

We think that in daily improvised conversations the problems emerge and change their character in the midst of the conversation. With reference to 'the bench' and also the experience with the OHS consultants, we think that this is of major importance. In improvised theatre and in organizational improvisation what emerges did not exist before but is created in the actors' relating to each other in the very moment (this argument will be developed in Chapter 4).

In their definition of spontaneity in organizations, Vera and Crossan say that it is 'extemporaneous, unpremeditated and unplanned'. They also incorporate flexibility and intuition, which they see as closely aligned to spontaneity and creativity. In their reflections about theatre improvisations, spontaneity is seen as a mixture of 'making do' and 'letting go', where the first emphasizes the creative part and the second the spontaneous part. They do not focus on how responding or re-acting is changing the meaning of what was just said. We think that they come to lack an understanding of the improvisational processes as such, and instead they end up talking around the issue. 'Improvisational theatre is about embracing the uncertain, trusting intuition, acting before thinking, adapting to circumstances, and working as a group in a process of creation' (ibid.: 731).

We come to see that Vera and Crossan think of theatre improvisation as something that primarily goes on in the individual, in line with the thinking of Schein. They write, 'when improvising, individuals flexibly respond to new circumstances, make exceptions to rules, and make subconscious use of their intuition to generate solutions rapidly' (ibid.: 734). This does not provide an explanation of the transformational processes that for us are so evident in theatre improvisation, and that we also find as a part of everyday ordinary conversation. They write, 'Collective improvisation is more than a sum of individual improvisations: it is the result of a close interaction among members of a group' (ibid.: 743), but they do not explain how this can happen.

We agree with Vera and Crossan when they mention that 'competition, power and status are often important factors affecting team dynamics' (ibid.: 743), and the next two chapters will explore this. They focus on the 'principles of agreement', referring to the importance among improvising actors of accepting the offers given by other actors. By blocking an offer you miss a chance to make the play evolve. However, they do not aim at understanding what actually happens when you accept an offer, which means that you run the risk of transforming yourself as a character, which in improvisational theatre is what the audience is waiting for.

Vera and Crossan find it important to 'define boundaries within which experimentation can occur' (ibid.: 740). They stress that there is no guarantee of a positive outcome of improvisation, but they find that it is necessary to learn the principles that help it to work (ibid.: 744). In the end this is the 'responsibility of the managers to influence the success of improvisation by managing contextual factors nurturing improvisational processes' (ibid.: 744). So, they see improvisation in organizations as going on in certain environments carefully defined and guarded by the managers. If we take seriously the unpredictability of the outcome of improvisation, which Vera and Crossan too understand as being very important, how can this be the case? How can managers 'ensure' these boundaries? We think that the managers also have to improvise, that managers cannot escape being a part of what is going on, and therefore also have to 'work live'.

In the next two chapters we will explore how we have come to understand the processes of improvisation from our experience of working with theatre improvisation.

References

Barrett, F. J. (2002) 'Creativity and Improvisation in Jazz and Organizations: Implications for Organizational Learning', in K. N. Kamoche, M. P. Cunha and J. V. Cunha (eds) *Organizational Improvisation*, London: Routledge.

Bastien, D. T. and Hostager, T. J. (2002) 'Jazz as a Process of Organizational Innovation', in K. N. Kamoche, M. P. Cunha and J. V. Cunha (eds) *Organizational Improvisation*, London: Routledge.

Boal, A. ([1979] 2000) *Theatre of the Oppressed*, London: Pluto Press.

Boal, A. (1992) *Games for Actors and Non-actors*, London: Routledge.

Boal, A. (1995) *The Rainbow of Desire: The Boal Method on Theatre and Therapy*, London: Routledge.

Carroll, A. (2005) *Skills4success*, Web page [Online] http://www.skills4success.net (accessed 9 June 2005).

Crossan, M. and Sorrenti, M. (2002) 'Making Sense of Improvisation', in K. N. Kamoche, M. P. Cunha and J. V. Cunha (eds) *Organizational Improvisation*, London: Routledge.

Cunha, M. P. E., Cunha, J. V. and Kamoche, K. (2002) 'Organizational Improvisation', in K. N. Kamoche, M. P. Cunha and J. V. Cunha (eds) *Organizational Improvisation*, London: Routledge.

Elias, N. ([1939] 2000) *The Civilizing Process*, Oxford: Blackwell.

Fonseca, J. (2002) *Complexity and Innovation in Organizations*, London: Routledge.

Gesell, I. (2005a) *Homepage of Izzy Gesell*, Web page [Online] http://www.izzyg.com/ (accessed 9 June 2005).

Gesell, I. (2005b) *A Ropes Course for the Mind: Building Teams and Communication One Improv Game at a Time*, Web page [Online] http://www.izzyg.com/Articles/Ropes.pdf (accessed 9 June 2005).

Hatch, M. J. (2002) 'Exploring the Empty Spaces of Organizing: How Improvisational Jazz Helps Redescribe Organizational Structure', in K. N. Kamoche, M. P. Cunha and J. V. Cunha (eds) *Organizational Improvisation*, London: Routledge.

Johnstone, K. (1981) *Impro: Improvisation and the Theatre*, London: Eyre Methuen.

Johnstone, K. (1997) *Improvisation og Teatersport*, trans. A. Boertmann, Gråsten, Denmark: Drama.

Johnstone, K. (1999) *Impro for Storytellers*, New York: Routledge/Theatre Arts Books.

Kamoche, K. N., Cunha, M. P. and Cunha, J. V. (eds) (2002) *Organizational Improvisation*, London: Routledge.

Kanter, R. M. (1977) *Men and Women of the Corporation*, New York: Basic Books.

Kanter, R. M. (2001) *Evolve! Succeeding in the Digital Culture of Tomorrow*, Boston, MA: Harvard Business School Press.

Kanter, R. M. (2002) 'Strategy as Improvisational Theater', *MIT Sloan Management Review*, Winter: 76–81.

Keefe, J. A. (2003) *Improve Yourself: Business Spontaneity at the Speed of Thought*, New York: J. Wiley.

Mead, G. H. ([1932] 2002) *The Philosophy of the Present*, New York: Prometheus Books.

Mead, G. H. (1934) *Mind, Self and Society from the Standpoint of a Social Behaviorist*, Chicago, IL: University of Chicago Press.

Mintzberg, H. (1973) *The Nature of Managerial Work*, New York: Harper & Row.

Schein, E. H. (1999) *Process Consultation Revisited: Building the Helping Relationship*, Reading, MA: Addison-Wesley.

Shaw, P. (2002) *Changing Conversations in Organizations: A complexity approach to change*, London, New York: Routledge.

Stacey, R. (2003) *Complexity and Group Processes: A radically social understanding of individuals*, London: Routledge.

Stacey, R., Griffin, D. and Shaw, P. (2000) *Complexity and Management: Fad or radical challenge to systems thinking?*, London: Routledge.

Streatfield, P. J. (2001) *The Paradox of Control in Organizations*, London: Routledge.

Vera, D. and Crossan, M. (2004) 'Theatrical Improvisation: Lessons for Organizations', *Organization Studies*, 25, 5: 727-749.

Weick, K. E. (1995) *Sensemaking in Organizations*, Thousand Oaks, CA: Sage.

Weick, K. E. (2001) *Making Sense of the Organization*, Oxford: Blackwell.

Weick, K. E. (2002) 'Improvisation as a Mindset for Organizational Analysis', in K. N. Kamoche, M. P. Cunha and J. V. Cunha (eds) *Organizational Improvisation*, London: Routledge.

Editors' introduction
to Chapter 3

In this chapter Henry Larsen, a consultant at Dacapo Theatre in Denmark, examines in detail a critical incident in his work with an organization and seeks to understand what is happening as small but significant changes are experienced. He suggests that at such moments there are shifts in the webs of power relations that constrain and enable particular situations of human organizing. He contends that what is critical to whether or not change occurs is how much spontaneity people find themselves risking in the face of power differentials which constrain novel responses while enabling familiar responses. He asks how the heightened sense of risk is to be understood and what makes invitations to spontaneity, invitations to act into the unknown, both difficult and crucial.

Larsen describes a scene from a consulting engagement with a small business wanting to improve the processes of knowledge creation and knowledge sharing in the company. He examines in detail what occurs as members of the company, including one of the owner-directors, become involved with the professional actors in the improvised action. He explores the different kinds of risk-taking involved for all concerned: for himself mediating between the active audience and the improvised play, for the professional actor, for the director who agrees to improvise with her, for his co-directors and management team watching and responding to what develops. Larsen argues that spontaneity, though experienced personally, is a social process. He explains the kind of changes that the theatre work stimulates as shifts in the patterns of social control. He proposes that the value of the theatre work lies in the way it enables small but significant shifts in power relations to be experienced live as mutually sustained identities are reconfigured.

He also examines the interplay of fiction and reality, the liberating as well as the constraining effects of 'truthful' characterization and relationships 'on stage' and the paradoxical emergence of surprising yet convincing developments as audience and players improvise together. This spontaneous emergence of 'truth' is actually not a moment of uncovering what was already known, but a new social 'recognition' of ourselves in our situation. It does not happen instantaneously; it happens in the movement of the improvisation as meaning emerges spontaneously and so identities are in flux as this is happening, the confusion and loosening of control, constituting the sense of risk. He argues that, far from being a useful stimulus to changes occurring later, the dramatic work creates immediate changes in the ongoing life of the organization.

It seems to us that the apparently small shifts Larsen describes, nevertheless experienced as significant among participants, change what is 'known' organizationally. This change comes about because changes occur in what can be talked about, how, when and with whom, and is thus highly relevant to the knowledge creation and knowledge sharing project.

3 Risk and 'acting' into the unknown

Henry Larsen

Prologue

On stage, Rosa, an actor playing a cleaner, comes into the top manager's office. She walks around, does some work, looks briefly at the actor playing the manager and starts to work again. The second time she passes him she looks at him more intensely. He is busy with his papers on the desk. She says, 'May I ask a question?' The manager, played by another actor, looks up, surprised. He was hardly aware she was there. He says, 'Of course', and she hesitates but then looks firmly at him and says, 'Why are you doing this?' 'Doing what?', he responds. 'Why am I not allowed to wear this logo any more?' She points at her chest. The manager hesitates, 'Your supervisor was supposed to tell you about that.' 'Haven't you been a part of the decision?', she asks. As the words start to flow, Rosa becomes gradually more direct: 'Are you not satisfied with my work?' The manager takes a look at his papers on the desk and gives her a short glance. He picks up his papers. On his way out he says: 'You need to talk with your supervisor about this.' The scene ends with Rosa standing alone in the office.

We are working in a scout's cabin in the woods. Eighteen managers, from a company which manufactures furniture, are gathered here today. The company's thirtieth anniversary will occur next year. Among the participants are three partners who jointly own the company. Until four years ago it was run by a senior partner, who suddenly died. The oldest partner is the CEO, the youngest is responsible for a successful production department and the third is responsible for human resources (HR) management. The last-named is the one who had contacted us.

We had been working in the company nearly two years earlier, and it had been a huge success. We had been doing workshops with smaller groups and had in this way worked with all employees and most of the managers. At that time they were defining 'values' for the company, and they wanted us to work with theatre to create a dialogue about this. In preparing this work, actors and consultants talked with people in the production department and became aware of a particular pattern. The management sensed that major changes lay ahead to ensure the firm's survival as a furniture company in Denmark, without knowing exactly what these changes would be. So, their strategy was to shift away from a management culture which largely told people what to do towards one which encouraged employees to take on more responsibility within a framework of values that would result from our work together. What we realized – which may not be surprising – was that people in production were waiting for the managers to tell them what they had planned for the future, thinking that they had just not told them yet and finding the work with values rather weird. We had rehearsed a piece of theatre that had been used in all the workshops, followed by joint improvisation about the evolution of this fictitious situation. The scene we played had invited exploration of these differences in expectation, and within the company the work was seen as very successful.

So now we were invited to work with the managers about issues related to 'the sharing of knowledge'. The partner responsible for HR had invited us to several conversations about this, believing that the managers had to be more open with each other about the 'soft' part of management, about the difficulties each manager had in dealing with people. After the first meeting, things had been postponed and another half-year had gone by. In the end we decided that we should work over six days, gathering all the managers twice: first the front-line managers divided into two groups, then the top managers, including the three partners, following this initial work with workshops where we would mix the front-line managers and the top managers.

This is the third day in the scout cabin for the top managers. The two days with front-line managers had been difficult. We had played some stories we hoped they would find relevant but when they were asked to work with these stories, they avoided doing so and made comments like, 'The play itself is OK, but it does not help in any way.' Gradually we had realized that many were unsure about each other and especially about the partners. Many did not want to share knowledge with each other, and they particularly did not want to say things to the partners. In our work an important theme turned out to be the outsourcing of the company's cleaning. A decision to take this step had been taken a short time before we worked with them and had caused much uncertainty and criticism among the employees. The front-line managers were not told about the decision and some of them found themselves in a situation where they had to face angry workers without knowing what had happened. They found themselves giving unsatisfactory answers, and some of them had even told their people that this could not be true. The company had never dismissed people in its history, and some people had been working in the company from the very beginning. We discussed our experience from the first two days with the HR partner and he reacted very strongly when he heard about the problems. He expressed his disappointment. He had been personally responsible for enacting the decision, and felt that he had ended up with a very good arrangement for the cleaners with the company that was taking over the work, so it was very difficult for him to accept the critique that he had heard indirectly this way.

Now we are introducing this theme for the higher management. As we role-play the situation with Rosa, I am watching the three partners. The HR partner is very nervous, in contrast to the others. In the middle of the play, the oldest partner chats with the person beside him, and what goes on obviously does not capture his interest. A minute before, he had risen from the chair and walked around. The youngest partner too does not seem to be very engaged, although his reactions are less impolite. It is the first time I have seen all three partners together, and in this moment I come to think that the HR partner took a risky decision in inviting us to do this. His reasons had been something like 'If the company is to survive and be able to continue production in Denmark, people need to be better at working together and willing to share their knowledge with each other.' He had invited us because he had realized that for some reason this was not happening, or at least not enough. At this moment there does not seem to be much support from his partners and this is, perhaps, not only about the theme we are working with; it might also be about the way we are working, namely using theatre improvisation.

In the same moment I understand why the HR partner reacted so vigorously when he heard about the reaction from front-line managers regarding the outsourcing of the cleaning. He is well known in business circles for taking a socially responsible approach, for instance by bringing in people of foreign origin, and disabled people. Perhaps these initiatives, although passively accepted by the other partners, were not seen as very important by them; perhaps this made it more difficult for him to accept all the complaints from the rest of the company. This goes through my head while Rosa is standing in the office alone. I ask the participants how they feel about the way the manager handled the situation with Rosa. Nobody says anything for a short moment. 'Of course he will have to give her an explanation. He can't just leave,' says the youngest partner, the one in charge of production. He expresses himself as if this is obvious, as if it is a fact, and as if just saying this will rectify the situation. He is obviously used to people not challenging him when he speaks like that. I invite him to try it on stage. He had not expected that. I interpret the look on his face as, 'Oh, that's the game you are playing; why didn't you tell me?' It is obvious to me that he would have preferred to stay seated but he gets up. I get the idea that it would have become too embarrassing for him to say 'no' to this invitation.

On stage he becomes extremely nervous. He tries to joke, says that this is just theatre; it is completely unrealistic with all these people watching. Rosa asks him the same question as before, and he tries to answer, still with all his focus on the people in the audience. It is obvious that he really would like to get out of this situation and I am very close to intervening. Then Rosa (or Lena, the actor) leans over and tells him not to take any notice of these people. There are just the two of us, she says. She does not allow him to respond, because Rosa then takes the initiative and begins to ask questions that demand answers, questions like 'Are you not satisfied with the quality of my work?' 'Are we too expensive?' 'Will it become cheaper after the outsourcing?' Gradually he begins to answer her questions. She questions again until she understands the answers. He becomes more and more engaged in really answering her, and the more he concentrates on that, the better it goes. When he leaves the stage Rosa obviously understands a bit more about the outsourcing. People applaud him and he seems fine, although still a little shaken.

What I want to explore in this chapter is how theatre, as a form of consulting, can play a part in organizational change. I will argue that experiences of theatre such as the one I have just recounted change power relations and identity and that this *is* organizational change. Our work with theatre provides an invitation to risk a shift in power relations by encouraging spontaneity. Others have worked with 'organizational theatre', but a prevailing theme in these approaches is to see theatre as a laboratory, a test run for later 'real' work (Jagiello, 1998; Meisiek, 2002; Gulløv, 2003; Schreyögg and Höpfl, 2004). I will argue that this is not so. Change happens as an integral part of the theatre process.

Contributing to organizational change: improvised theatre influences power relations

For Boal (1998, [1979] 2000), well known for his work with forum theatre among socially deprived groups in Brazil, the audience is 'the oppressed', and he creates a 'we' situation with a kind of universal consensus in the audience about a common oppressor. The point of Boal's work is to offer people resources with which to change the relationship of oppressors and oppressed. In the story with which I introduced this chapter, the audience were managers, and if we were to take Boal seriously, we would define the cleaner as the oppressed and the manager as oppressor, inviting the audience to identify with the oppressed; or we would look for external oppressors recognized by both parties; or we would reject working with this audience of managers by seeing them as oppressors. I do not see any audience as an entity with one set of structural power relations, and in the example above we were working with conflicts between different participants in the audience. The cleaner herself is not the problem, but the situation initiates an important theme about ethics and what it means to be a manager. Boal assumes that when an audience actively engages in a play by proposing solutions, this serves as a test run for problems that are encountered in real life. It is usually assumed that engaging in solving the problem motivates the participants to engage in similar problems in real life (Boal, [1979] 2000; Meisiek, 2004). This assumes that the real work goes on afterwards, implying that the work we are doing in the prologue is not creating change at the time. However, I saw an actual shift happening in the relations between the youngest partner and Rosa, which had implications for the ongoing relations with the others in the room. I call this, in itself, a 'change', not merely a test run for something to take place later. Rosa may exist only on stage, but the relation between her and the youngest partner is happening live; it influences, and involves a shift in, his relations to others. For Boal, the role of the consultant, known as the joker, is to ask Socratic questions through which ideas already present in the audience are expressed. In the above story, however, new ideas emerged that had not existed before. In my position as what Boal would call 'the joker', the most critical moment was when I sensed new ideas about what was going on between the three partners, ideas that inevitably influenced my way of reacting to the emerging situation. I see myself as participating in an ongoing process, not trying to bring forth a pre-existing idea. Consequently, my role cannot be that of a 'midwife'; that is, giving birth to what was already conceived in people's minds, which I see as a consequence of Boal's position.

In contrast to the 'before and after' thinking of Boal, I have found inspiration in the view of theatre improvisation developed by Keith Johnstone (1981, 1999). For him, improvised theatre emerges through actors re-acting to their co-actors. Lena reacted to the nervous partner and her response changed significantly from the way she had responded to the actor who played the role before. This time Rosa assumed a much higher status in response to the new situation. In doing so, she could not know how the partner would react and so she had to improvise. Since she is a skilled and experienced actor in this kind of work, she knows that usually something worthwhile will happen as a result of taking this risk.

I have come to see an organization not as something 'being there' in a reified sense, but as 'being there' in the way we talk and relate to each other. We are patterning communication and action as we interact with each other in daily life, in the same way that a scene emerges during theatre improvisation. By being involved in local interactions in daily life, referred to by Stacey *et al.* (2000) as complex responsive processes, we create and recreate our identity at the same time, just as the relationships among actors in theatre improvisation create their roles and the situation through continuous reaction. Obviously, this involves spontaneity, since we cannot predict what we are supposed to respond to and so we do not know in advance what to answer. However, in many situations we control our spontaneity and find others and ourselves in situations that we think we have been in before, patterns we can recognize. I had never seen the youngest partner before and I could not know how people would respond to his remarks about Rosa just before I asked him to go on stage. However, in the situation I did not feel surprised that nobody commented on his remarks. I sensed a controlling of spontaneity in their bodily reaction and I felt it myself. It felt natural that nobody reacted, and I think that the patterning of extremely constraining interdependency that emerged in this situation felt familiar: people had experienced this before. Stacey talks about spontaneity not as pure impulse but as 'a skilful, reflective capacity to choose different responses, developed in the life history of interaction' (2005b: 13). Here the passivity felt like a skilful response, in a way the only natural reaction. There seemed to be no opportunity for others to choose different reactions, perhaps because of a fear of exclusion and because the current pattern of power relations between them felt too dangerous to challenge. What I noticed was a specific way of talking, and people's bodily reactions too were familiar to me. This changed when the youngest partner went on stage. The usual, familiar patterning of interdependent collusion was not possible in this situation because he actually meets Rosa in front of all the others and because he cannot get away with ignoring her. He has to participate in spontaneous activity where he is seen and recognized in a new light. This creates a new situation, and, being a part of it, people make sense of this instantly, and not as a separate later process.

So, working with theatre has contributed to a change in the patterning of conversation. Exactly how this will emerge we cannot know. Introducing fiction, like Rosa, contributes because the fictitious situation had become 'real' or 'true'. Even if the youngest partner had refused to go on stage, that too could also have initiated a significant change in the configuration of power relations among the people present. As it becomes obvious to me that this involves the relation between the partners, it takes a new turn. Momentarily my view changes about the partners' relationship and the difficult situation that the HR partner found himself in. This emerged very powerfully, and I think that I was not the only one to see it. In the flow of all this, I sensed a conversational change, enabled by the risk-taking of the youngest partner's response to the gesture of Rosa/Lena. In using the notion of risk-taking here, I understand *risk as spontaneity in the face of power differentials*, spontaneity not as pure unreflected impulse, but as finding oneself reacting in an unforeseen way, not carefully planned but still against the background of an awareness of the other and others in a particular social context. And I understand what is going on here as the detailed way in which organizational cultures actually change.

The youngest partner was completely surprised and embarrassed but found a way of participating. From taking a detached position, he suddenly became involved in a way that he would or could not escape or fully control. By engaging in how difficult it actually was to talk with Rosa in front of his fellow partners and managers, he changed in his way of understanding the outsourcing theme. That was what I experienced, and I also think that something happened in the experience of other participants. By this I do not mean that he changed his *opinion* about whether the decision to outsource was wrong, but he realized that talking about it was much more important than he had anticipated. Also, I sensed a shift in the power figuration between the partners. The HR partner was in a difficult position and he was nervous. As the youngest partner was relating to Rosa, his relationship with the other partners was also in play and was changing at the same time. So when the youngest partner became involved, it immediately created another power configuration between them. As I said before, this is how I experienced it, but in the unspoken response from people I sensed that others too were making fresh sense. By this I do not mean that what happened on stage had consequences that are to be understood sequentially; that is, something happening first on stage that later had an impact upon relationships. The change is experienced by me and also by others immediately. Of course, I cannot know how this will turn out later. Still, I perceive this as essential for organizational change.

One immediate consequence was that later the same day the older partner asked for some time to talk about negotiations on work conditions which were planned to take place in the near future. He took his time to explain what the intentions were and why he, as the CEO, thought that this was important and what the managers needed to appreciate. He had not intended to talk about the negotiations before coming on this day, but a shift had taken place in his way of thinking because he had now become more immediately involved, and this had influenced his thinking about the responses he could expect from the others. He had been able to see things from their perspective and this had changed his decision about when it would be appropriate to involve them in the plan. I came to think that the three partners usually spent a lot of time agreeing with each other and they made an effort to present themselves in clearly defined roles to the rest of the organization. Here the other participants came to see one of the partners acting live. Even though it was on stage, it was as convincing as if it had been going on in real life: it actually happened, and could not be undone. It was realistic and powerful, and it may therefore have changed their thinking about the reactions of one of the owners. Also, they had the opportunity, as I did, to experience a relational change between the partners going on live.

As we continued the work in the next three sessions we saw a shift in the way people responded to each other. At the last session the HR manager participated. We asked for stories, and one brought up difficulties about handling Monday absenteeism. The managers felt powerless because the HR manager had implemented rules about giving people warnings, and they felt that these warnings had no effect. On stage we played a situation where a manager felt ridiculed by an employee who had repeated days of absenteeism, and the manager felt that the employee was laughing behind his back. We played the situation on stage, and more managers were able to recognize the feeling of what they saw. In the end the HR manager went on stage, playing the front-line manager, and a discussion emerged about the intention of the warning and how the HR manager thought that it could be followed up. Obviously it was possible for the front-line managers to talk with the HR manager in a way that had not been possible some months before.

Although the work was easier for us in the later sessions we felt that people found the work hard. In training sessions they were used to being given learning tools, but our sessions had been very different. After the last session the HR manager asked us to write our version of what had happened. In the conclusion we wrote:

> When we started the work we felt that people were thinking: 'What can I say to whom and what will the consequences be?' We sense that this gradually is changing towards: 'What are the consequences of saying nothing?' We see this development as a good sign.

After several months the HR manager had still not responded. The way of talking about change that I try to explore here, and that we had endeavoured to discuss with the HR manager, is significantly different from the way he and his colleagues were talking about more clearly 'managed' processes. I imagine that there may have been a kind of amplification of a hesitation that had been present from before we started. What developed from the disturbance of balances of power experienced as we worked together with the improvised scenes? We found ourselves hesitating to contact people 'behind the back' of the HR manager to inquire further, so here power configurations were influencing our actions and constraining our spontaneity. So, the shifts in power relations I have drawn attention to, which I am suggesting always carry the potential for organizational change, may or may not ripple out further. The potential may or may not be realized. As long as people repeat the patterning of responses to each other, the power configurations are recreated over and over. Change comes from sensing small shifts and responding spontaneously. In the following I will explore how we can understand spontaneity not as an individual phenomenon, but as an interdependent activity among people, linked to power relations.

Understanding spontaneity

In gesturing and responding, we are constantly creating images and narrative fragments of what other people are thinking. I have explored some of the images I created in the midst of the work with the furniture company. Mead talks about this as 'taking the attitude of the other', where the 'other' is both particular others and generalized others, those of one's social milieu (Mead, 1934). At the same time, we find ourselves responding in ways that we cannot predict, because the response, and the response to the response, take place as the present, and will therefore inevitably involve spontaneous action – some kind of action that is not predictable, even to oneself, although, in varying degrees, recognizable when it happens. I think that we are very often trapped when we are trying to make sense afterwards, because we tend to confuse the familiarity with what happened with the idea that we can anticipate that exactly this would be the outcome. As we are responding to others we are also responding to ourselves, namely the attitude we have taken of the other. Mead calls this the 'I–me dialectic'. Self, for Mead, is this continuously ongoing process, taking place individually as the 'I–me dialectic', and socially as gesturing/responding – in effect, the same process going on at the same time. I have argued how the processes of gesturing/responding I was involved in were influencing my way of understanding the relationship between the involved people and consequently also my way of understanding my role.

In conversation, intention/gesture includes enacting the interplay of past experience, and at the same time this intention changes as one relates to the other and to the attitude of the other as one experiences it. As the situation emerged, my view of the HR partner changed, which immediately influenced my intention and my way of reacting to the situation, because my view of my role also changed. So, relating spontaneously goes on in an interaction where one takes the attitude of the other, and this in turn shapes and transforms one's view of oneself. This happens spontaneously as one finds oneself saying and doing something that is not planned.

Spontaneity as an interdependent activity

With reference to Johnstone and Mead, I see spontaneity as an activity of relating without being in control of the situation, meaning that one acts before being able to tell why. I find myself intervening in the play before knowing why I do so. When I think that I need to know, I have found that my intervention becomes sterile, stifling the flow of interaction as I wait until I have formulated my reason for interrupting to myself. The spontaneous reaction is influenced by what I remember, and what I perceive, but I react before I am able to consciously account for all this.

In this work I have become aware that I am reacting spontaneously to the tiniest bodily gestures of other participants. One cannot hold back a certain bodily reaction (such as a smile or a frown); another responds and this in turn calls forth further response. A kind of bodily resonance is going on, and I notice that this iteration happens at such lightning speed that one reacts independently of being able to express the response in words. This is in line with Stacey's views on the sharing of knowledge when, referring to Stern (1985) and Damasio (2000), he concludes, 'Instead of thinking about sharing something going on in the brain, one might think of bodies resonating with each other, yielding empathic understanding' (Stacey, 2003: 118). In the work with Rosa these kinds of processes go on constantly. When the younger partner said that Rosa needed an explanation, I reacted to the patterning of bodily reactions that immediately followed. Here it was not a smile following a smile, but a holding back of spoken response that I reacted to.

I have come to see spontaneity as making sense together, paradoxically by staying with the situation and by acting surprisingly into it, searching for mutual recognition. Spontaneity is manifested between people not only as activities involving talk and language, but also as bodily reactions that are equally part of conversation. Gergen (1999) talks about 'rhythms of conversation', by which he means bodily interactions. Recently I have become aware of new brain research that sheds new light on the physical aspects of communication. We have certain neurons, called mirror neurons (Gallese *et al.*, 1996), that recognize and associate intention with certain patterns of action, especially hand and mouth movements. These neurons recognize movements made by other humans at the same speed as movements made by oneself (Wohlschlager *et al.*, 2003), and much more quickly than thought, indicating that on the neural level humans are essentially reacting socially (Ferrari *et al.*, 2003). McNeill links this research with Mead's understanding of humans as essentially social:

'One's own gestures can activate the part of the brain that responds to intentional actions, including gestures, by someone else, and thus treats one's own gesture as a social stimulus' (2004: 14). This explains spontaneity as social activity; where in the emergence of patterning one surprises oneself as well as the other. I understand the 'I' as social here because the unpredicted response to 'me' can be seen as generated in the social activity.

As I mentioned, I reacted to the patterning of unspoken conversation that immediately followed the youngest partner's statement, without knowing exactly why I reacted, and of course also without knowing exactly what I would be doing as I found myself doing it. However, I argue that this does not mean that my spontaneous reaction takes place separately from reasoning and experience; rather, it is a part of them, as what it means to make sense together.

Invitation to spontaneity

Just as we can attempt to control conversation by making an effort to control the act of responding, I think that we can also offer themes that serve as *invitations to loosen control*. I think that this notion of invitation to spontaneity is ubiquitous among humans. We find ourselves invited to spontaneity when we are in the middle of a gesture–response interaction that *disturbs our assumed view of the other* – the image/illusion of the people we know. One can recognize an invitation to spontaneity as interaction where one has only fuzzy expectations in the patterning of conversation. In contrast to spontaneity itself, invitations to spontaneity can be partly planned. In our work with theatre we are deliberately trying to encourage mutual spontaneity, and I see our activity with theatre as an invitation to spontaneity. When our actors play a piece of theatre that involves people, like the one with Rosa, it is inviting people to spontaneity. I experience that being involved in spontaneity and any invitation to spontaneity is *risky*, because I cannot know how people will react, and therefore I cannot know how my relationship with them will emerge. Understanding spontaneity as a social activity means that it becomes essential in understanding novelty, creativity and innovation. Therefore, I find it important to try to understand the nature of this risk.

As I have developed my argument it is obvious that the nature of the risk has to be linked to breaking anticipated patterns in communication. This links with Mead when he explores social coherence in terms of *social control.*

The notion of social control

Taking the attitude of the other enables social control to emerge, according to Mead:

> The human societies in which we are interested are societies of selves. The human individual is a self only in so far as he takes the attitude of another toward himself. In so far as this attitude is that of a number of others, and in so far as he can assume the organized attitudes of a number that are cooperating in a common activity, he takes the attitudes of the group toward himself, and in taking this or these attitudes he is defining the object of the group, that which defines and controls the response. Social control, then, will depend upon the degree to which the individual does assume the attitudes of those in the group who are involved with him in his social activities.
>
> ([1932] 2002: 195–196)

It is because each of us can take the attitude of the other that social control emerges, because we take into account how the other will perceive our reaction. So how do we explain why it can be so difficult to invite spontaneity and why it often feels so risky? In the furniture company the front-line managers hesitated to talk with the owners, and also with each other when it came to themes about how to do one's work as a manager. Even the top managers became quiet when one of the owners spoke. How do power relations affect social control?

As a part of the earlier work with values in the furniture company, we had been working with people from the shop floor of the factory. The actors play a situation where a man – Fritz – had taken a place that, according to the agreed rotation system, was Carla's. When Carla asks him to move, he refuses. The day before, he was moved from the workplace where he should be according to the plan, and now he does not want to be pushed around. On stage the actors played out a possible gossiping conversation between Carla and one of her friends, Lisa. I asked the audience: What would be the next thing Carla and Lisa would do? Chatter about how stupid he was, they said. And next? I asked. Tell somebody else about him, they said. We played that on stage. Somebody would tease him in the canteen, they said. We saw that. What is happening? I asked. No reaction. So what can he do? I asked. He can piss off, somebody said. Nobody tried to protect him. Fritz becomes excluded, an outsider. Nobody in the audience was allowed, or allowed themselves in this situation, to articulate his perspective. How is this to be interpreted from Mead's understanding of social control as taking the attitude of the other? Why can it be so difficult for people in that situation to take Fritz's attitude? How can we understand the nature of this? Were they unable to see his perspective, or were they just afraid of speaking it aloud? How are we to fully explain the anxiety that I felt among people in this situation or why the processes of human relating are often felt as risky?

Power as dependency

In his writing Elias has explored the emergence of civilization as we know it, and for him power is essential in understanding this:

> We depend on others; others depend on us. In so far as we are more dependent on others than they are on us, more reliant on others than they are on us, they have power over us, whether we have become dependent on them by their use of naked force or by our need to be loved, our need for money, healing, status, a career, or simply for excitement.
>
> (1998: 132)

Elias understands this dependency as essential for human activity; consequently, power is a human condition, and for Elias it makes no sense to talk about any human relationship without taking power into account. Elias disagrees with any idea of the individual as a self-contained unit, calling this concept *homo clausus*, and also uses the image of 'thinking statues' (Elias, 1991). Elias is talking about 'we' identities, by which he means that people sharing the same view of other people become a group. Individuals who do not share the same meaning run the risk of being excluded from the group.

Elias says that groups define themselves in the process of including and excluding others. People find themselves belonging or not belonging. Elias and Scotson (1994) studied the relations between a group that moved to a new housing estate in Winston Parva, a community with an older estate. Conflicts, hostility and gossip proliferated. Elias and Scotson note that avoiding open contact with others is extremely important for the group's ability to create and sustain its identity:

> It is symptomatic of the high degree of control that a cohesive group is able to exercise upon its members that not once during the investigation did we hear of a case in which a member of the 'old'

group broke the taboo of the group against non-occupational personal contact with members of the 'new' group.

(1994: xxxix)

Elias focuses on the kind of self-control that is exercised in groups, and shifts are anxiety-provoking. In the light of this it is not difficult to understand the audience's reaction to the story about Fritz referred to in the previous section, and the manager's hesitation towards the partners in the furniture company. People did not want to challenge the prevailing opinion because they feared exclusion, an anxiety that can be present without necessarily having to be explicit for the people involved. Perhaps they were not even able to see the situation from Fritz's perspective. In their study of Winston Parva, Elias and Scotson make the point that:

As a matter of course, members of an outsider group are regarded as failing to observe these norms and restraints. That is the prevailing image of such a group among members of the established group. Outsiders are . . . experienced as anomic.

(ibid.: xxiv)

Maybe people were unable to hear Fritz's argument about the unfairness he had experienced the day before, as he could be considered anomic. I cannot know; but, judging from the way people reacted, I sensed that this was the case for many of the participants, as Elias observes about the established group from Winston Parva.

It is not only in what we would perceive as the powerful groups that this 'we' identity is played out. I read recently an interview with a black man who noticed the repression of people he had lived with in his childhood. Reading books and listening to specific types of music was 'whitish behaviour', and being black you simply did not do things like that when living in that particular community. It is not difficult in this light to see how ideology is produced by gossip and other ways of creating a 'we' identity. Stacey refers to Elias when he says:

Ideology is thus a form of communication that preserves the current order by making that current order seem natural. In this way, ideological themes organize the communicative interactions of individuals and groups. As a form of communication, as an aspect of the power relations in the group, ideology is taken up in that private role-play, that silent conversation, which is mind in individuals.

(Stacey, 2003: 125)

This gives a clear framework for understanding the relational nature of power and creation of identity, groups and ideology. As Stacey says, it goes on in public as conversation among people, and in private as silent conversation of the individual. However, while Elias is fully aware that the emergence of these patterns is unpredictable, he does not focus on how this happens in the ongoing relationship, in the micro-interactions, as he does not recognize the importance of spontaneity in the sense that Mead does.

Joas (2000) also finds a need to focus on power and exclusion in understanding identity. However, he establishes a split between dialogical processes based on Mead, which, he finds, form identity, and power processes – including violence and exclusion – which, he finds, stabilize identity. In a chapter about values and norms in organizations in another volume in this series, Stacey (2005a) argues against this dualism, since both the genesis and the stabilization of values arise at the same time and by way of the same processes of communicative interaction and power relating. Stacey points out that there are no universals outside human interaction, which is not the same as saying 'anything goes', because any generalizations and idealizations are constantly particularized in a specific interactive situation involving negotiation of conflict and power relating (see Chapter 6). This is in line with my attempt to find a way of understanding how spontaneity and power are intertwined in these processes.

Before continuing with this, I will now briefly examine other ways of looking at power in organizations as a way of putting Elias's work into perspective.

Mainstream understanding of power

Dahl defines power as follows: 'A has power over B to the extent that he can get B to do something that B would otherwise not do' (1957: 202–203). Mintzberg (1983: 4) defines power as 'the capacity to effect (or affect) organizational outcomes'. Kanter (1977) refers to classical physics in her definition of power as potential energy. Kearins (1996) notes that such views are founded on the assumption that power is a commodity that can be possessed. She comments that the majority of authors of books on organizations convey the idea of power as something that can he harnessed and used for the good of the organization.

Mintzberg (1983) mentions that the word 'power' lacks a convenient verb form, forcing us to talk about 'influencing' and 'controlling' instead. However, in his book there is no focus on power as a temporal activity, as it is restricted to an exploration of structures that can be recognized as holding potential power. Pettigrew (1977) conceptualizes the dynamics of an organization as individuals or groups that make claims upon the resource-sharing system of the organization, which is regulated by power. He conducted detailed examinations of power in organizations, for instance in 1972 exploring the control of information in a company's decision process, and in 1998 exploring power in fifty boardrooms (Pettigrew, 1973, 1979; Pettigrew and McNulty, 1998). Pettigrew and McNulty (1998: 201) argue that it is time to augment the structural methods of the agency and managerial hegemony theorists by an approach to power dynamics that is jointly contextual and processual. However, the term 'processual' here acquires a specific meaning, since power is basically still seen as a commodity linked to the structure. The contextual and processual part is thus treated in terms of the individual 'will and skill' to exercise it.

Pfeffer (1981, 1992a, b) sees organizations as political battlefields, and considers the interests between opposing power structures to be what develops organizations. Pfeffer also understands power as a potential force (1992a: 14). For him, power is a tool for getting things done, deliberately chosen by the individual to enforce intentions already there. However, Pfeffer partly accepts uncertainty by saying that 'the consequences of our decisions are often known only long after the fact, and even then with some ambiguity' (1992b: 37). But he finds that we as individuals have to run that risk, because without power nothing could be done.

In conclusion, none of the above-mentioned approaches meets Elias's notion of power as dependency. Instead, they tend to understand power as what Elias would call an amulet, something to hold: the potential power is 'there'. And there is no focus on the importance of spontaneity.

Linking power and spontaneity

Reading Elias, I have come to understand power as dependency that constrains the relation; paradoxically, the same constraint also enables the relation. I have come to see changing power relations as inherently linked to the emergence of spontaneity. This is risky, and on the basis of the work of Elias, I understand the nature of this as the risk of exclusion and anxiety concerning the loss or fragmentation of identity.

To act spontaneously is both conscious and unconscious, in the sense that one is not at that moment fully aware of, or in control of, one's action. Spontaneity is not to be chosen freely or independently by the individual; it is relational activity involving bodily gestures that our brain is able to 'read' – and to which we attribute intention – with lightning speed (Ferrari *et al.*, 2003; Gallese *et al.*, 1996; Wohlschlager *et al.*, 2003). The creation of a 'we' identity as described by Elias, by processes of including and excluding, by gossiping and by creating ideology, is the basis for understanding the creation of power relations and understanding the nature of the risk that is linked to spontaneity and invitations to spontaneity.

Power and spontaneity: a paradox

As power relations are about dependency, they are a fundamental aspect of all human relations, which paradoxically constrain and enable the relationship at the same time; and in this dependency we recognize the other as well as ourselves. However, this dependency is not static or just 'there' – together we create and recreate it as we are moving continuously, both in patterns we can recognize and at the same time in new patterning that is unfamiliar to us. As we take steps together, the spontaneity involved challenges the power relations, and this is why spontaneity and invitations to spontaneity are felt to be risky. One can recognize spontaneity as a sense of liveliness in relating in the present as one becomes challenged and confused in taking the attitude of the other. Moving together is thus a process of spontaneity in which we are recognizing or not recognizing each other. This is the creation of dependency that is a power relation. So, paradoxically, spontaneity and invitations to spontaneity are creating and challenging power relations at the same time as power relations are making it risky to act spontaneously.

In the furniture company the youngest partner ends up on stage with an actor playing a cleaner, with the task of explaining to her why her job was going to be outsourced. As a member of the audience, he had insisted that she was entitled to a decent explanation. He had expected this to settle the situation, and I could sense from the bodily reaction of the other participants that they also had expected this to be the last word on the matter. So, he was surprised when I invited him on stage to give her an explanation, and he definitely did not want to go. But had he rejected my invitation, he would have lost power in the eyes of his partners, the rest of the participants and in his own eyes; so he accepted the invitation, which then turned into a highly improvised situation, again shifting power relations. Working with people from the shop floor, there was a very strong theme of exclusion of people who did not behave according to norms. However, in the following work some of the newcomers protested against this. They were able to identify with Fritz, the character on stage who was excluded, because they had the same experience from their daily life, and as we played the situation they ran the risk of speaking up.

My interpretation of both situations changed as a part of the spontaneous activity. When the youngest partner went on stage, this changed my view of the HR partner, the one who had invited us to work with the company, since I came to understand the risk he had been running by inviting us. I also gained insight into the way the partners related to each other and to their employees. I note that this insight came to me in the midst of spontaneous action.

I will now continue by reflecting about the particular risk-taking that is a part of working with improvisational theatre. In other words, how can we see our work in the light of this discussion of spontaneity and power?

Fiction and reality in theatrical performance

Usually theatre is seen as fiction, opposed to reality. We need another language for the kind of work we are doing with improvisational theatre, which I see as paradoxically fictitious and real at the same time. I will now turn to the anthropologist Schieffelin, who reflects on the relation between the illusory, or fictitious, and the real in performance.

Schieffelin (1998) notes that Western culture has a specific tradition of understanding performance such as theatre. In the Aristotelian tradition we think of spectators as living in the real world, in contrast to the actors on stage, who create a virtual or imaginary 'reality'. In this context, acting means make-believe, illusion, lying. Although we acknowledge that performance has the power to affect us, still it remains no more than an illusion, a simulacrum. Schieffelin questions this way of thinking. It is, in his words, 'a significant epistemological stumbling block' in understanding performance. He sees performance as central to human activity; every act has an expressive dimension and he says that 'The central issue of performativity . . . is the imaginative creation of a human world' (ibid.: 205). Schieffelin says that performance cannot be understood solely as a result of conscious intent on the part of the performer. It can only be understood as a relationship. While the burden of success is usually laid on the performers, the real location is in the relationship between the central performers and others. Thus, Schieffelin sees performance as a contingent process in which both the performers and the audience are constituted within the relationship between them. Performance is always interactive and fundamentally risky. This is close to the way I understand the relationship between our actors and the other participants we are working with.

> Where Western assumptions align their relation between performer and spectator with relations like signifier/signified, text/reader, illusion/reality, and deceit/authenticity, activity/passivity, manipulative/straightforward, they conceal important moral and epistemological judgments that undermine anthropological discussions which make use of Western performance ideas in an unexamined way. It is for this reason that it is important to make the relationship between the participants and others in the performative events a central subject of ethnographic investigation.
>
> (Schieffelin, 1998: 204)

He suggests that the dichotomies that we usually take for granted – for example, that what happens on a stage is illusion as opposed to reality – are misleading. This challenges us to find other ways of understanding the opposites. Rather than seeing simple dichotomies, we have to recognize theatre as, paradoxically, both illusionary and real.

Schieffelin's argument is very close to my understanding of the communicative act and I see clear links to the way I have described my understanding of what happened in the episode described at the beginning of this chapter. The responses people give to the apparently illusory theatre are real, and through their responses they co-create the fiction as real, while at the same time paradoxically it is fictitious. Reading Schieffelin reminds me that with theatre we are communicating in a special way, by performing. He is very clear about how the traditional Western way of understanding theatre is misleading, because it splits fiction and reality in an unfruitful way. Schieffelin notices that there is always a risk in performing because of the unpredictable nature of what emerges. For Schieffelin, as an anthropologist, there is only one valid approach, namely, to work towards understanding the nature of the particular relationship in the performance. Schieffelin sees performance as a powerful, expressive dimension of strategic articulation, which does not mean that what comes across is purely consciously intended. The power in this is that it is co-constructed and not a simulacrum. This makes me think of theatre as a strong gesture, that our work is a powerful way of communicating, if the process of creating theatrical work is accepted by the participants and audience alike, as in the situation with Rosa. In the acceptance that can be seen by the engagement of the participants it becomes real, because their response is real, live in the situation. This encourages me to explore theatre more fully: how can I understand the particular form it takes, the power relations between participants in creating and working with fiction, and the risk taken by actors in performing in these situations?

Common to the actors' backgrounds are two main influences that I see as important for identifying oneself as an actor in the Dacapo Theatre. First, there is the work of Konstantin Stanislavskij, perhaps the person who has meant most for Western theatre as we know it today; and second, the work of Keith Johnstone, who is known as the father of improvisational theatre. How do they talk about what it takes to create characters and relations on stage?

Creating convincing characters and relations on stage

Theatre in Western culture has been hugely influenced by Konstantin Stanislavskij, a Russian theatre person and writer. In a series of books (Stanislavski, [1936] 1989, [1949] 1994, [1961] 1989) he has described the work of the actor and how an actor can be trained. He died in 1938, but it is a striking experience to read him because I can recognize much of what I read from daily conversations with the actors I work with today. Stanislavskij founded a theatre in Moscow in 1898 and he worked with Chekhov's pieces, which have great emotional subtlety. He realized that the art of acting had to be renewed. He talked about creating 'truth' on stage. By this he meant that the spectators believe in what they see. The task was to make the spectator believe in the 'scenic truth', forgetting that it is a play and not actual reality (Stanislavskij, [1936] 1998: 244). This can easily be seen as being in line with the Western understanding of theatre that Schieffelin criticizes, which creates a split between what exists in real life and what you believe in on stage. But Stanislavskij expresses himself more subtly – for instance, by saying that you 'believe' in it as spectator. Believing is not simulacrum, and I read this as meaning that Stanislavskij acknowledges the involvement of the spectators, who want to believe in the scenic truth. The kind of theatre Stanislavskij was working with was very different from the interactive, improvised work that we do. For Stanislavskij, the rehearsal ended in a set piece, and the actors were supposed to find their roles and be able to play them in a convincing way with each other, day after day, and the audience members were expected to remain spectators. But I think that creating 'scenic truth' is also an essential part of our actors' work, creating a fiction on stage that can be believed in by all participants. I think that our actors find their identity as actors in their ability to go into this work.

Stanislavskij's influence has primarily been on the training of actors, and how to rehearse and develop roles in preparing a performance. He invented what is known as the 'method of physical action', also called 'the improvisational method'. In the early years, Stanislavskij wrote his most famous book, *Creating a Role* ([1936] 1998). Here he talks about creativity as belonging to the subconscious. The task is for the individual actor to make every effort to keep a mental pathway open to 'the creating subconscious', and it is possible to consciously grasp the subconscious by using mental techniques that stimulate the actor's subconscious mind (ibid.: 458).

In his later work he focused more and more on the importance of physical activity, physical movement, and also the actors' physically relating to each other. In rehearsals, Stanislavskij again and again focused on presence and physical action. Seeing the role not as given, not as something already 'there', but as something that needs constant work in the situation, Stanislavskij focused on improvisation. Even in the rehearsed and finished play, he would encourage the actor to appreciate disruption because this provides an opportunity to bring freshness into what may have become a well-rehearsed role.

Relating is not explicitly mentioned as being of importance, and it might seem as though the work is done by a single actor alone. It seems a kind of magic that it is possible at all, and Stanislavskij reinforces this impression by referring only to the actor's 'access to the subconscious' in understanding this creativity. However, in his praxis, Stanislavskij's method of physical action ensures that the work is carried out in a way that is almost entirely relational – for instance, by creating the role in improvisations with other actors. The focus Stanislavskij has on physical action is very important for the actors I know. This influences not only their work with the creation of fiction but all suggestions and ways of working, and this way of thinking is clearly a part of their identity as actors. Stanislavskij states that as an actor you cannot use other people's emotions, you can only draw on your own ([1936] 1998: 39). By playing a role, whose words he does not feel responsible for, it becomes possible for an actor to say things that would feel very risky if he were not playing a role. Characterization hides the actor as an individual, and, protected by this 'mask', he dares to lay open the most intimate corners of his soul (ibid.: 41).

Keith Johnstone acknowledges the work of Stanislavskij, referring to a situation in one of Stanislavskij's books where he asks an actor to go into a room. The actor objects, 'How do I know how to do this?', apparently needing some direction. Stanislavskij responds, 'Don't you know how to go into a room in an inn?' For Johnstone, this is about *status*: 'What I think he "knows" is that he will have to play a particular status' (Johnstone, 1999: 47). By status Johnstone means 'pecking order', which he says is always established among social animals, preventing them from killing each other for food. Status is a bodily reaction and humans are very aware of the way status differences are enacted physically. For instance, a calm head and a steady voice are typical of high-status behaviour, whereas turning one's toes towards each other, touching one's face again and again, not keeping one's head calm are low-status actions. Johnstone deliberately trains actors to assume a certain status and to respond immediately to the status they meet, by being able to change their own status. Of huge importance is the ability to change status. This was what I saw Lena do in the situation described at the beginning of this chapter. When she realized that the man was scared and could not concentrate, Rosa changed her status from low to much higher, to a cleaner who might not have been realistic if it had not been for this situation. This change in status was of great importance for what happened in their relations, and Lena was very aware of this.

About what you need to know as an actor, Johnstone says:

> I began this essay by saying that an improviser shouldn't be concerned with the content, because the content arrives automatically. This is true and also not true. The best improvisers do, at some level, know what their work is about. They may have trouble expressing it to you, but they do understand the implications of what they are doing; and so do the audience.
>
> (1981: 142)

What happens is unknown for the trained actor, yet paradoxically not completely unknown because he or she will have had similar experiences before. Johnstone is pointing to the difficulty of being able to improvise with recent experience still in mind, without ending up with repetition or failing to react in a lively way in the situation.

Taking risks working as an actor in the Dacapo Theatre

In the light of this, what can I find to be important for taking risks in the actor's performing?

As I already have mentioned, what we are doing is

- Not theatre in the sense of Stanislavskij, because of the high degree of improvisation.
- Not improvised theatre in the sense of Johnstone because in his kind of improvised theatre the actors are creating what happens on stage much more among themselves. In our work the audience constantly give cues and their spontaneous reactions guide the actors.
- Not forum theatre in the sense of Boal either. However, what does apply from Boal is his notion of staying with realism on stage, in the sense that the audience accept the co-constructed work not only because they are amused, but because they accept it as realistic. It is by staying with this that it becomes serious work, even if it is at the same time often very funny.

To do this our actors work hard to continuously be able to take on the attitudes of participants from the client's organization in their acting. This makes the performance of improvisation very realistic, and the sometimes unrealistic turn that 'theatre sport' can take is almost absent from our theatre.

Conclusion

In contrast to other ways of understanding organizational theatre, I describe power as key. I see power as relational and it is in the midst of power relations that we find our identity. Change is consequently a change in power relations, which inevitably is risky because your identity, understood as a process of mutual recognition, is at stake.

Similarly, I can account for the way that working with theatre contributes to change precisely because of its ability to change power relations.

Because we work with fiction, people are more willing to risk their status, either by involving themselves or by accepting what takes place on stage as true or convincing. Working with theatre is not a laboratory situation, the consultant is not managing the process and the actors are not doing work that other participants see merely as simulacrum. While I have just mentioned that theatre creates fiction, this is a paradox: however fictitious, it is at the same time real, because participants are co-constructing what is going on and accepting it as true, and thus it is influencing the power relations among them. How this will turn out cannot be predicted in advance.

Theatre, then, can be powerful as a part of organizational change. I have been part of a team where we have increasingly developed our ways of working, and our relations to clients have been changing. Actors obviously play an important part in this work, and their ability to co-create fiction that is seen by other participants as true or convincing is of the utmost importance. By looking at the theatre tradition they are a part of, I see key themes that seem important for their ability to run the risk of creating truth on stage. Amid this is the importance of creating fiction, because actors experience the emotions and reactions they find themselves in on stage as their own, so the fiction serves as a protection for them as well as for the other participants.

References

Boal, A. ([1979] 2000) *Theatre of the Oppressed*, London: Pluto Press.

Boal, A. (1998) *Legislative Theatre: Using Performance to Make Politics*, London: Routledge.

Dahl, R. A. (1957) 'The Concept of Power', *Behavioral Science* 2: 201–215.

Damasio, A. (2000) *The Feeling of What Happens*, London: Vintage.

Elias, N. (1991) *The Society of Individuals*, Oxford: Blackwell.

Elias, N. (1998) *Norbert Elias on Civilization, Power, and Knowledge: Selected Writings*, Chicago, IL: University of Chicago Press.

Elias, N. and Scotson, J. L. (1994) *The Established and the Outsiders: A Sociological Enquiry into Community Problems*, Thousand Oaks, CA: Sage.

Ferrari, P. F., Gallese, V., Rizzolatti, G. and Fogassi, L. (2003) 'Mirror Neurons Responding to the Observation of Ingestive and Communicative Mouth Actions in the Monkey Ventral Premotor Cortex', *European Journal of Neuroscience* 17, 8: 1703–1714.

Gallese, V., Fadiga, L., Fogassi, L. and Rizzolatti, G. (1996) 'Action Recognition in the Premotor Cortex', *Brain* 119, 2: 593–609.

Gergen, K. J. (1999) *An Invitation to Social Construction*, London: Sage.

Gulløv, T. (2003) *Communicating Ambiguous Information* [Online] http://www.lok.cbs.dk/images/publ/Thomas%20Gullov.pdf (accessed 31 October 2004).

Jagiello, J. (1998) 'Organisational Theatre of Continuous Learning: The Application of the Forum Theatre Technique to Continuous Improvement', paper given at Second Euro CINet Conference, 'From Idea to Reality', Enschede, the Netherlands.

Joas, H. (2000) *The Genesis of Values*, Cambridge: Polity Press.

Johnstone, K. (1981) *Impro: Improvisation and the Theatre*, London: Eyre Methuen.

Johnstone, K. (1999) *Impro for Storytellers*, New York: Routledge/Theatre Arts Books.

Kanter, R. M. (1977) *Men and Women of the Corporation*, New York: Basic Books.

Kearins, K. (1996) 'Power in Organisational Analysis: Delineating and Contrasting a Foucauldian Perspective', *Electronic Journal of Radical Organization Theory* 2, 2.

McNeill, D. (2004) *Thought, Imagery and Language*, book to be published [Online] http://hci.ucsd.edu/coulson/260/McNeill8.pdf (accessed 25 May 2005).

Mead, G. H. ([1932] 2002) *The Philosophy of the Present*, New York: Prometheus Books.

Mead, G. H. (1934) *Mind, Self and Society from the Standpoint of a Social Behaviorist*, Chicago, IL: University of Chicago Press.

Meisiek, S. (2002) 'Situation Drama in Change Management: Types and Effects of a New Managerial Tool', *International Journal of Arts Management* 4: 48–55.

Meisiek, S. (2004) 'Which Catharsis Do They Mean? Aristotle, Moreno, Boal and Organization Theatre', *Organization Studies* 25, 5: 797–816.

Mintzberg, H. (1983) *Power in and around Organizations*, Englewood Cliffs, NJ: Prentice-Hall.

Pettigrew, A. (1973) *The Politics of Organizational Decision-making*, London: Tavistock.

Pettigrew, A. (1977) 'Strategy Formulation as a Political Process', *International Studies of Management and Organization* 7, 2: 78–87.

Pettigrew, A. (1979) 'Power, Innovation and Problem-Solving in Personnel-Management', *Personnel Review* 8, 3: 47–48.

Pettigrew, A. and McNulty, T. (1998) 'Sources and Uses of Power in the Boardroom', *European Journal of Work and Organizational Psychology* 7, 2: 197–214.

Pfeffer, J. (1981) *Power in Organizations*, Marshfield, MA: Pitman.

Pfeffer, J. (1992a) *Managing with Power: Politics and Influence in Organizations*, Boston, MA: Harvard Business School Press.

Pfeffer, J. (1992b) 'Understanding Power in Organizations', *California Management Review* 34, 2: 29–50.

Schieffelin, E. L. (1998) 'Problematizing Performance', in F. Hughes-Freeland (ed.) *Ritual, Performance, Media*, ASA Monographs, London: Routledge.

Schreyögg, G. and Höpfl, H. (2004) 'Theatre and Organization: Editorial Introduction', *Organization Studies* 25, 5: 691–704.

Stacey, R. (2003) *Complexity and Group Processes: A radically social understanding of individuals*, London: Routledge.

Stacey, R. (2005a) 'Values, Spirituality and Organizations: A Complex Responsive Processes Perspective', in D. Griffin and R. Stacey (eds) *Complexity and the Experience of Leading Organizations*, London: Routledge.

Stacey, R. (2005b) 'Social Selves and the Notion of the "Group-as-a-Whole"', *Group* 29, 1.

Stacey, R., Griffin, D. and Shaw, P. (2000) *Complexity and Management: Fad or radical challenge to systems thinking?*, London: Routledge.

Stanislavski, K. S. ([1936] 1989) *An Actor Prepares*, trans. E. R. Hapgood, New York: Routledge.

Stanislavski, K. S. ([1949] 1994) *Building a Character*, trans. E. R. Hapgood, New York: Routledge.

Stanislavski, K. S. ([1961] 1989) *Creating a Role*, trans. E. R. Hapgood, New York: Routledge.

Stanislavskij, K. S. ([1936] 1998) *En Skuespillers Arbejde med Sig Selv*, trans. E. Rovsing and E. Rostrup, Copenhagen: Nyt Nordisk Forlag.

Stern, D. (1985) *The Interpersonal World of the Infant*, New York: Basic Books.

Wohlschlager, A., Haggard, P., Gesierich, B. and Prinz, W. (2003) 'The Perceived Onset Time of Self- and Other-generated Actions', *Psychological Science* 14, 6: 586–591.

Editors' introduction
to Chapter 4

In this chapter Preben Friis, an actor and director at the Danish Dacapo Theatre, continues to explore the value of 'fictional' presentations of 'reality' in working with improvisational theatre to support organizational change. He points out that the common management discourse advocates the creation of future vision (in effect a fiction), assessment of current 'reality' and planned movement towards the desired future. This separates fiction and reality conceptually and in time, whereas he shows that his work takes fiction and reality as paradoxically at work simultaneously in the acts of imaginative social construction by which we make sense in narrative form of what we are doing together. Like Larsen in the previous chapter, he concludes that fiction and reality come together in the social act of recognition of 'truthfulness' in improvised scenes. He asks how such 'truthfulness' emerges and what it permits.

Friis inquires into the experience of being more or less 'present'. He makes the interesting contention that it is when we are affected, moved, altered by what we perceive that we are experienced by others as most 'present'. When we remain unaffected we are likely to be experienced as less 'present'. This leads him to surmise that it is self-in-movement, rather than self clinging to familiar forms of identity, that leads to the experience of being present and thus contributes to the intangible quality often referred to as 'presence'.

How does this link to understanding improvisation? Friis explores his own experience as a theatre director working improvisationally with a troupe of actors towards a public performance. This gives him personal insight into the dilemmas of taking up a position of authority in a situation where all are acting together into the unknown. Again he notes the paradoxical experience of being in control and not in control at the same time. The innovative work produced in this way necessitated risk – he was unable to be ahead of the game, and his authority and influence with the group depended on his ability to retain spontaneity. If one compares his account with Larsen's, it is interesting to see how power differentials potentially constrain spontaneity however they are experienced, and it is spontaneity in the face of constraining power relations which is often recognized as acts of leadership that enable movement and change. Friis's analysis of what happens as his improvisational work becomes institutionalized into method and best practice is insightful: increased anticipation and predetermined order, created by making sense retrospectively, afford a comforting sense of being in control, of being able to transfer knowledge and implement an approach, but the quality of the product diminishes.

Finally, Friis takes up Shotter's (1993) ideas about civil society. Shotter argues that personhood is achieved by a sense of playing a part in the creative sustaining of a community as a 'living tradition' (ibid.: 163), a highly contested process. Friis proposes that it is in taking up the challenge of being fully present to the live negotiation of what is involved in being a full member of one's community or organization that one participates influentially in organizational and personal change.

4 Presence and spontaneity in improvisational work

Preben Friis

- ● **The Grindy Company**
- ● **Fact and fiction**
- ● **Theatre improvisation**
- ● **Teaching improvisation**
- ● **Social interaction as improvisation**
- ● **Spontaneity**
- ● **Presence**
- ● **Improvising in organizations**

At the Dacapo Theatre we use theatre as a mode of consulting to organizations. Improvisation has always been a key aspect of our work. However, when we started ten years ago we mainly did three-hour workshops, and the first half of the workshop was a straightforward theatre performance, while the second half was improvised work using the issues and situations arising in the performance. One of our first performances has so far been performed over five hundred times, but despite this obvious success, our work has gradually moved away from performance towards more and more improvisation. Today we may work for a day with the staff, or some of the staff, of a company without using any rehearsed theatrical material at all. This movement is not the result of a deliberate decision but has happened gradually over time as a result of many small decisions from job to job. This led us to reflect on why we have developed in that direction, and these reflections probably helped us take a next step in another situation. So we did not plan it; we did not wake up one morning and realize that we had moved away from performance to more improvising. Rather, it has been a process of interwoven action and reflection. This movement has taken place despite demands from clients, which could have influenced us to stay with the use of theatre performances. Consider an example of such a demand.

The Grindy Company

We were invited to a meeting with the human relations (HR) director, the production manager, a team leader and a few workers from the production department at the Grindy Company. This company had recently been taken over by new owners who demanded that production be doubled in three years, which required changes in ways of working. The HR director had invited us because we had worked for the company a few years previously at a conference for all seven hundred employees. We had performed a forum play but we were also involved in helping them to create a conference with life and energy, instead of the usual speeches by the management. 'The employees still talk about that conference,' the HR director said. He had not been a member of the organization at that time but had heard about the event and now wanted us to do something similar, something with the same effect.

> 'We need the employees to live up to our new corporate values. We need them to share their knowledge with each other, to be open to change, to build bridges to customers on all levels and to be proud of working for the company. But we've had two strikes in production lately. So we think it would be good to gather everybody together again in a conference to make them understand all this and we think theatre might be a good way to do it.'

It is obvious what the HR director had in mind in involving the Dacapo Theatre. He wanted an effective tool with which to rapidly transform the attitude of the employees. I think he knew from experience that telling the employees how they should think and behave would not provide the result he wanted, and instead of questioning his approach to the problem, he looked for a stronger means of communication. On hearing about the event three years ago, when the theatre had had an impact that people still remembered, he may have thought that he had found what he was looking for.

I can understand his argument. This is how theatre and film are talked about. I was watching a Clint Eastwood Western on television. The story went something like this. The people of the village used to live in peace but a gang of villains had ruined the peace and left the inhabitants in fear and agony. They did not know how to deal with the new situation. Then the hero comes riding in. He immediately analyses the situation, or instinctively knows what to do. It is going to be a tough fight, which may cost lives, but what has to be done has to be done, and if the hero is Clint

Eastwood he will do it almost alone. He never wastes time on a dialogue with anybody or even a brief explanation of what he is up to or has done. He takes the leadership through his actions, risking his life for a cause which is not his own but that of the villagers. He is a strong personality with simple, but always the right, answers. And when the battle is over and peace is re-established, the inhabitants understand that the hero was right, that they had acted stupidly, and had they not acted in so cowardly a way in the beginning, the problems would have been solved a long time ago with less pain and loss.

The parallels with the Grindy situation are clear. They too used to live a quiet life (at least, that is how it looks now that it is changing). Then the competition in the world market became tougher. New owners came in with new ideas about the method and speed of production and how to organize the work. But the pressure from outside and all those new demands are confusing for the employees; they become afraid that they will not be able to cope and may be fired. So instead of facing the new situation and trying to find out how to deal with it, they hide and look for ways to defend themselves individually or in small groups. And the production level drops. This is when it would be nice to have Clint Eastwood, alias the HR director, come in and show everybody how to solve the problems and establish a new order with a new quiet life (not as quiet as it was, but still much quieter than the current mess, where you do not know whether you will survive in the company). And this is where he sees a theatre performance with the right 'message' as a useful tool.

Why do we not want to do what he asks and give him the tool he thinks he needs? In order to answer this question I will look at the interplay between the fictions created by the theatre and the actual life of the audience.

Fact and fiction

We used to distinguish clearly between television programmes such as the news and discussions about political, social and scientific issues, which were considered to be *factual programmes*, and others such as films, theatre and other entertainments, which were categorized as *fiction programmes*. The factual programmes were supposedly addressed to detached spectators in a manner that enabled them to make more 'objective' judgements, while fiction programmes were expected to involve people in more 'subjective' emotional experiences. Of course, factual programmes did get some people very involved and fiction programmes often left many people untouched. However, the general aim of producers of fiction was to present their stories in a way that would arouse maximum emotional involvement, whereas producers of factual programmes aimed to present the facts for the viewers' own reflections and avoid manipulation.

In a post-modern society where 'the truth' or 'reality' is no longer taken for granted and all perspectives are supposed to be equally valid, there is a tendency, however, to persuade people to believe in your perspective not by arguments, but by 'staging' yourself or your perspective in an emotionally manipulative way. Whether you are dealing with fact or fiction is no longer important. What is important is that you get your way.

So, from films and TV the HR director may have come to think that manipulation through creating a fiction could be a quick way to change people's beliefs. But the message he wants to send to the employees is that they need to become more independent and responsible. To believe that this can be achieved through one-way communication is, I think, illusory. If the employees are not treated like independent and responsible people, how can they ever begin to act more independently and take more responsibility? Of course the 'message' can have an impact on the audience but not an impact you can control in the way the HR director seems to believe you can.

Watching a theatre performance, the audience are all the time detached from the action in the play. They are experiencing it from the outside and it has only an indirect influence on their lives even though they are present in the room where the action takes place. It is a live performance and so in theory they could interfere with, and influence, what is happening, but they don't. Why not? Probably because there is a social contract, which most people adhere to, that determines the roles of those on stage and the role of being a member of an audience. It is not a contract made explicitly between the people present at the beginning of the performance but it is recreated every night in every performance. In many ways this resembles the old relationship between the management and the employees in a company. The managers were the actors who led 'the performance' and the employees were to follow and behave according to the 'rules'. Even though this pattern is still played out in many subtle ways, it is no longer the main way of communicating in companies. One-way communication is gradually being replaced by two-way communication. Information is replaced by dialogue.

This is a challenge to us as theatre people working in change management. A theatre performance can be seen as one-way communication like film and television, but the great advantage of theatre is that it takes place 'live': the actors and the audience are present in the same room and thus there is the possibility of two-way communication, which means that the audience will move from being spectators to becoming participants. But if the audiences are becoming participants in a two-way communication, it means the actors lose the possibility of repeating the script they have rehearsed when preparing the play as a theatre performance. Instead the actors will have to improvise. The advantage of improvising with the audience is not only in creating a two-way communication, but also that we mix fact and fiction in a different way.

One of our latest projects illustrates this. A group of senior managers from different companies wanted to work with what they called 'the unspeakable'. It is very hard for a senior manager to find anyone to talk to about very difficult, sensitive problems. We asked the group of managers for a story we could work from but they could not tell us because the stories they wanted to work with were too delicate to tell. From our own fantasy we then improvised a two-minute scene about a CEO who comes home late after a meeting with the board. He is absent when talking with his wife and obviously deeply troubled about something he does not share with her. We stop and ask the audience what is bothering him and they have no difficulty in creating stories of what may be troubling him. In a joint process they create a challenging scenario he would not be able to talk about to anyone. And so here they are talking about what cannot be talked about. They are not doing this in the hypothetical way of talking about difficult issues in principle. Although the story they are creating and playing out on the stage is a fiction, it is also real because they have all put dilemmas from their own lives into creating the story. We check with them constantly to find out whether what we are playing is what they consider important to work with. Without this reality, the fiction would have been uninteresting, and without the fiction, the reality would have been too difficult to talk about. So it is fiction and reality at the same time, in an inseparable way. If you collapse the paradox into either pure fiction or pure reality it will not work. In this universe of simultaneous fiction and reality I saw that people were able to stay present and so be altered by their experience. They managed to share personal experiences of a kind it had not been possible to share before except in closed circles. New ways of enabling people to speak about the unspeakable emerged as we worked. This means that change does not occur as a result of the work, but rather that the work itself constitutes change. Change occurs as movement in the web of relations between people in an improvisational mode rather than primarily through planned actions.

This is an important difference compared with what the HR manager wants. He is maintaining the more usual view in which change is seen as a separate, planned transition phase between the reality of the current state and a fictitious future state. When a leader or manager creates a vision of a 'future state', I would say he is creating a fiction in which people can recognize themselves and which helps them to handle the anxiety of the unknown future. However, this fiction really is fictitious in that everybody knows that what happens from now on will change the perception of the future and that the 'future state' will never become reality. Fiction and reality are in this example divided in time as two different stages in the process of change.

I have come to think that splitting *fiction* and *reality* in this way is not useful and I claim that we do not split *fiction* and *reality* in the way we work with theatre improvisation but, rather, work with both in a paradoxical way. Our job in using theatre as a mode of consulting is not to persuade anyone to take over the pictures, plans or values of the management by performing an emotionally involving story with a more or less open 'message'. Instead, our job is to take part in meaning-creating processes in which no one, least of all us, can know what the outcome of the process may be. For this a theatre performance is not helpful. If we want to use theatre, it must be created in the moment as part of the process – we must improvise.

But what does it mean to improvise? Theatre improvisation sheds some light on this question.

Theatre improvisation

There are a number of different ways of thinking about improvisation in the theatre. For example, Rudolf Penka and his partner Gerhard Ebert, who were among the leading teachers in Brechtian theatre in East Berlin in the 1970s, saw improvisation as a way to develop new theatrical material, which then had to be repeated and fixed to be useful. 'An improvisation is an improvisation until it's been fixed. From reiteration to reiteration the improvised is becoming more and more fixed' (Ebert and

Penka, 1985: 79). The play is 'there' to be found, and improvisation becomes a stage in the development of the play, but the creative process takes place within very limited frames. This way of thinking about the aim of improvising is also found in organizations. The usefulness of improvising is to learn ways to do something better. Out of your experience you decide how you are going to act in the future. This is making a best practice.

Viola Spolin, the grand old lady of American improvisational theatre, writes:

> [T]here is no right or wrong way to solve a problem, and . . . the answer to every problem is prefigured in the problem itself (and must be to be a true problem) . . . how a student-actor solves a problem is personal to him, and, as in a game, he can run, shout, climb, or turn summersaults as long as he stays with the problem.
>
> (1963: 20)

So this is improvising as problem-solving, which means that before you start improvising you have defined the boundaries: this is the problem and the answer is predetermined, although still unknown, because it lies enfolded in the problem. The freedom of the improviser is only the road to the answer.

I am still not quite happy about the way improvisation is explained here. Keeping some kind of control seems to be important both for Ebert and Penka and for Spolin in the way they explain and use theatre improvisations. However, it is important to acknowledge that you cannot stay in control when improvising. This is essential in understanding the nature of improvising. You are not in control of what is happening – which does not mean you're out of control. You are paradoxically in control and not in control at the same time. Trying to explain what I mean by this, I will describe my experience of teaching improvisation.

Teaching improvisation

Many years ago I was asked by a Danish amateur theatre organization to conduct a two-week course called 'From Improvisation to Performance'. I accepted, and wrote a few lines about the importance of knowing the different stages in the method of creating a performance from improvisation. Weeks later, when I was preparing myself for the course, I realized that I did not have a clue what the different stages were. I knew about improvising and I had some experience in doing theatre from four years of drama school and five years of acting, but what the logical or obvious steps from improvisation to a performance were, I could not figure out. Reading about it did not help me. So, when I met the twenty participants, I told them I did not want to give them a manual, which they expected, because I thought it important to experience the different stages before systematizing them. They accepted that.

So we started improvising, and after two entertaining and intensive weeks we had three very interesting performances. In the feedback on the last day, the participants praised me for dropping the manual and allowing them to experience the method, which was obviously so clear in my head. I was exhausted but happy and felt that I had learned a lot. When I was asked to repeat the success the next year, I was convinced I could do it even better since I now had a clear idea of a method. But I was wrong. The next year the course reached nowhere near the quality and fun of the first year. I agreed to do it a third time, now knowing from experience both what to aim for and what to avoid, but it turned out even worse and so I stopped. I had a clear feeling that the decline from success to disaster was no coincidence. I could not blame it on the participants or anything in the context. The blame was on me somehow. But I could not figure out why more experience and more knowledge seemed to lead to less and less ability. As I looked back, trying to picture what I was doing over the three courses, some differences became clear to me.

The first year was extremely hard work. I was scared to death because I felt I did not know what I was doing. I was desperately trying to find out at least what the next two steps in the work might be, but again and again I found myself asking the participants to do something without knowing why. I remember clearly those moments when we had finished something and it was obvious to everybody that we had to proceed to the next step. Often, I would call a five-minute break, hoping that I would know then what to do. And I would come back and feel blank and chaotically full of contradictory ideas at the same time. As I then began to speak, I would hear myself telling them what to do. In those moments, I felt like two different persons, one speaking and one listening, and if I had to say which of them felt more like me, it would be the listener. When I finished speaking, the participants would usually throw themselves into the work and I was relieved they did not ask too many questions, and so the two persons melted back into one. As the days passed, I began to realize that I could usually make meaning of what I had asked the participants to do once they had done it. It felt really awkward only knowing in hindsight what I was doing. I wanted to be ahead of the participants but I was not. It felt as though all of us were experiencing 'the method' simultaneously. The different stages in creating a performance from improvisation slowly came to life in front of my eyes and all I could do apparently was to help make sense of what was happening and then call that 'the method'. It was extremely frustrating, yet it worked fine. When I consider this experience today, I would say that I was improvising my work as it developed. And I would say that I was not in control of what was happening; yet obviously I was also not completely out of control. Rather, one could say that I was paradoxically in control and out of control at the same time.

The first year was very frustrating and extremely hard work, but I learned a lot. I think it is interesting to notice how I handled this experience, how over the next two years I turned improvised work into 'best practice'. I think I did this trying to regain control, which meant I lost the quality of the first year. Or I could say that by trying to stay in control, I lost control. Between the first and second years I was wondering who was the creator of 'the method', since I felt it was not me. And why was the second year such a failure when I obviously knew a lot more than the first year? I think what happened for me between the first and the second year might be what Shotter describes when he explains the four steps in what he calls the 'ex post facto fact fallacy' (1993: 85), which means that we create the meaning of our actions retrospectively:

1. Firstly a situation is described which, although we do not realize it at the time, is *open* to a number of possible interpretations.

It is obvious that when we started the work it could develop in different directions. There are, of course, many ways to make a performance from improvised scenes. I intuitively chose to do it one way but could have chosen from a number of others.

2. We are, however, then tempted to accept one of these descriptive statements as true.

Having chosen a next step and seeing it work well, I believed that I had made the right choice, which in a way was true, but I forgot that there might have been many other possible right choices.

3. The statement then 'affords' or 'permits' the making of further statements, now of a better articulated nature, until a systematic account has been formulated.

The first choice narrowed the possible next choices but also helped me see the direction in which a next step could emerge. And after some time I could begin to see the way the work developed as a system with an inner logic in the choices I made.

4. The initial interpretation (already accepted as true, of course) now comes to be perceived, *retrospectively*, as owing its now quite definite character to its place within the now well-specified framework produced by the later statements.

And after the course I wrote everything down as a nine-step manual on how to make a theatre performance from improvisation. I forgot that each step had developed out of the very first step and that each following step had been created in a specific situation so complex that at the time I had not been able to take it all in. It was a method of my own making, or of joint making by the participants and me, but I saw it as something that was also true outside the context in which it was developed. It became a formal system, which created a sense of logic, order and completeness. I knew of course that this was just one 'method' out of many 'methods' to create a performance from improvisation. I was seeing the method as a map and as I was preparing myself for second year, the map became more and more detailed. The more I worked on it the more convinced I became of the excellence of the method.

'However, the trouble is, once "inside" such systems, it is extremely difficult to escape from them to recapture the nature of our original, open and indeterminate thoughts, the thought to do with the system's development' (Shotter, 1993: 85). I think this covers very well what happened to me. I was sitting by myself developing the method without realizing that this way of thinking about the method did not '"afford" or "permit" the formulation of questions about its relations to its socio-historical surroundings' (ibid.: 86). It became a self-referential system that I did not question because I had seen it function very well. And it did not occur to me that the context in which it emerged, the socio-historical surroundings, played an important part. I was convinced that I could draw out the methodological essence from a very complex experience, which had involved many other people, and make that into a system, which could then be applied to other 'socio-historical surroundings'. I believe this is how we create 'best practice', and that we turn to 'best practice' because we want to stay in control and know where we are going.

But in order to 'know where we are going' in a play or conversation, we would have to be able to define the outcomes before entering the play or conversation, and this would split the process into two separate parts, namely, the preparation and the definition of outcome, and the implementation. I think this is how I worked in the second and third years. The outcome was that the participants should learn 'the method', and if they did not react positively to what I was teaching them, I would see this as either their fault because they were resistant to learning something new, or my fault because I was not explaining it well enough. In both cases I would have to go back one step and re-establish rapport to get them back on track. This may be an effective way of communicating *if* you know what you want and you know you are right. My experience is that this is very rarely the case (except for Clint Eastwood). I thought I knew what was right for the participants to learn. I never questioned that – only the way I was teaching it.

However, in the first year, I had no clear outcome and plan, but anyway I had to make a move and see where that took me. And since I could not solve the problem of what to do next by analysing or by reading a manual, I had to invent or create the next step on the spot. But where did I get the ideas to create the next step except in response to the participants? Seeing what they were doing, how they were responding to my suggestions, was the source I could draw from. So I became extremely observant and sensitive to what was happening.

When I say I was not ahead of the students it is true and not true. I did not have experience in doing a course like this but I had much knowledge and experience in theatre and improvisations. So I had some intention of where the work should be going, of course, but after each suggestion made, I had to see the response before being able to make the next suggestion. Often the response was surprising, going in a completely different direction from the one expected. Sometimes this was problematic because it did not develop the work and then I had to ask them to do something else. But sometimes the response led to completely new ideas, which changed my concept of where the work should be going because this was an even more interesting direction and so we pursued that.

Improvising is often talked about as the opposite of planning. In a planned process you try to foresee the end result and you think through each step towards this end result. In an improvised process you are acting into the unknown. You have an intention of where you want to go but you have to react to what is happening at each step, which may lead to a change in your intended direction. As work situations become more and more complex, the separation between planning and implementing plans becomes an illusion. My experience is that many managers repeatedly find themselves in situations where they have to make decisions in the absence of prior knowledge. They create the knowledge by making the decisions. In those situations, planning will not suffice and a different way of moving forward is required. One of our clients sends its leaders on a course called 'path-finder', implying that walking the usual roads is no longer enough. But it also implies that paths exist; you just have to find them. However, I see clients in situations where there are no existing paths. They have to create them, as they are moving forward towards an end which is steadily moving. Under these circumstances, I believe that the ability to improvise is necessary. Actually, I would say you cannot avoid it.

Social interaction as improvisation

I am beginning to get a different understanding of what improvising means. Instead of seeing improvising as a skill, something you need to learn and if you learn it you will be more able to improvise and if you do not you will be less able, I begin to see it as *the social interaction emerging between people all the time*. Our conversations and bodily communication as gesturing and responding are an ongoing improvisation created moment by moment. When we improvise, we are spontaneously responding to each other's gestures, and thus we do not know the full meaning of what we are doing until we have done it. The meaning emerges through the process of having intentions, acting and getting responses. This is a social process, where we are creating meaning together in what we are doing in the act of doing it.

Improvising leads to both repetitive actions and novelty. The paradox of improvising means acting in two apparently opposite ways: being skilled and experienced in what you are doing, and at the same time acting spontaneously. This is knowing and not-knowing simultaneously. Whether the emphasis is more on the knowing or the not-knowing varies from situation to situation and from person to person. If the emphasis is more on the knowing, if you are mainly acting on the basis of your experience, what you have already planned, how you usually do things, then you are more likely to stay with repetitive actions. If the emphasis is more on the not-knowing, the spontaneous actions, the possibility for transformation and novelty is greater. I think this is clear in the narrative about teaching improvisations. The trouble with defining improvising as 'the social interaction emerging between people all the time', however, is that it is so broad a statement that the question is whether it still makes sense to say that improvising is essential to our work. Why should improvising be helpful in change processes in organizations if we are improvising all the time anyway?

I think the answer to this question is that it is essential to our work exactly because we do it all the time. When we have gone through a process of change and creation we can always analyse it afterwards and explain it in an orderly way, as I did after the chaotic process of teaching improvising – but you cannot use it as a blueprint for the next process, as I also showed. So, even though we are planning and preparing, making contracts and agreements, a change process will always be improvisational in nature, and we have to take this experience seriously as a basis for our work. So, it is not a question of whether we improvise or do not improvise; the question is how much we try to control our improvising or how much we are willing to run the risk of not being on top of what we are doing. Do we dare to trust that meaning will emerge as we are spontaneously and skilfully working our way forward?

Spontaneity

Spontaneity is an essential part of improvising, so I will explain how I understand spontaneity.

I was playing a man called Benny in a mental institution. He has a hangover and is concerned only with finding a plastic bag and leaving. He takes somebody else's bag and empties it on the floor. The staff of the institution try to calm him down and to make him give the plastic bag back. But now he looks for his sweater. He does not respond directly to the staff but it distresses him that they are talking to him all the time. Suddenly he grabs a sweater on a chair, saying: 'I'll take yours!' and he leaves. As the actor, Preben, I was very surprised when the character, Benny, took that sweater. In my immediate memory after Benny had taken the sweater, I (Preben) was not aware that I (Preben) had seen the sweater before I (Benny) grabbed it. I think this was a spontaneous action. I have a clear sense of what spontaneous means but find it difficult to define, so in order to help me define it I look it up in a dictionary: 'Spontaneous: Happening or arising without apparent external cause; self-generated.'

This is not how I understand it. It is not self-generated. I am not doing what I am doing out of the blue – it is connected to the situation and it is a response to what has been happening. I look in another dictionary: 'Spontaneous: Arising from natural impulse or inclination, rather than from planning or in response to suggestions from others.' My action is not suggested by others; it is also not planned. I would say it is arising from an impulse in a moment influenced by what has been happening so far and my intentions for the future. And I am acting on this impulse without reflecting or considering the consequences.

I look up 'impulse': 'Impulse: A sudden desire, urge or inclination . . . a driving force producing a forward motion.' Reading this makes me want to look up 'desire', 'urge', 'inclination' and 'force'. But I do not, because I know I will end up going round in circles. And I think it describes quite well my experience of the situation. I had a sudden desire, urge or inclination to take the sweater, and this desire became a driving force, which produced a forward motion, which was to grab the sweater and leave. But as an explanation of what spontaneous means it is not precise enough for me, because between the sudden urge and the forward motion I could have reflected and made a decision and then I would not call it a spontaneous action. And I am not too sure that spontaneity is acting on impulse. If the spontaneous action were just based on impulse, it would be as George Herbert Mead says: 'If there were only "a word and a blow", if one answered to a social situation immediately without reflection, there would be no personality . . . any more than there is personality in the nature of the dog or the horse' (1934: 182). So, if I reacted on an impulse without any kind of reflection, I would have no personality. So, there is reflection involved in the spontaneous action. However, the reflection that occurs is intuitive. What I mean by this is that one does not have a full or complete grasp of what one is doing as a whole that one is conscious of. Rather, the acting into the beginnings of such a 'grasp' serves to develop it, in a way that one continues to sense as one continues to act. I would say, then, that I understand spontaneity to be an *immediate reaction based on intuitive reflections*, where immediate means that time is important, reaction means that it is relational, a response to a gesture, and intuitive reflection means that the reaction is rooted in the social experience of the person, yet not as a 'whole' fully present in consciousness prior to the moment of acting.

My concept of spontaneity derives from theatre, where it is essential to distinguish a spontaneous reaction from a rehearsed reaction in the process of acting. Good acting comes when you have rehearsed the play, but in the moment of performing it you are spontaneously recreating the play on the basis of the experience from the rehearsals. Expressing this idea in another way, you could say that you put aside the conscious controlling of the actions and leave it to the body to remember what you have to do according to the storyline, which gives you the possibility of 'being present' and acting spontaneously. This will bring the character to life. Returning to the story of Benny taking the sweater, I would say this was a spontaneous action to the extent that I did not know I was doing it until I had done it. This links to Mead's explanation of the emergence of self as a dialectic process between 'me', which is socially constructed by taking the role of 'the other', and 'I', which is the response to the 'me'.

> The 'me' represents a definite organization of the community there in our own attitudes, and calling for a response, but the response that takes place is something that just happens. . . . When it does take place then we find what has been done.
>
> (Mead, 1934: 178)

It is this aspect of spontaneity, namely, that it is only in hindsight that you can *find what has been done*, which creates the possibility of novelty in which you spontaneously create something that is not known from what is already known.

Presence

It is not easy to define 'presence' even though every actor will have some perception of what it means.

Eugenio Barba from the Odin Theatre prefers to use 'body-in-life' rather than the term 'presence', suggesting that being 'in the moment' is not just about mind, but also about body. He talks about the principle of opposition and the concept of 'energy in time'. 'Altering the normal equilibrium of the body creates . . . a "dilated body". Just as our pupils dilate in darkness . . . onstage the actor appears larger, more defined and more present' (Callery, 2001: 87). I think this 'principle of opposition' is important. It is the same principle you find in conflict, in dilemma, in paradox. So, being present does not mean you are in balance or tranquillity, rather that you are in a process of opposing forces, which creates energy. Conflictual situations offer the possibility of movement and change if you stay open. Avoiding those situations may create tranquillity but will inevitably lead to a lack of energy and development.

Callery adds one further dimension of presence, namely, 'truth', meaning: 'Whatever you do on stage, never be indifferent.' And this points to 'presence' being relational; it is not only what you are, but also a way of relating to other people in a situation. So, 'being present' includes having a heightened bodily energy and awareness of what is going on, using your senses, actively listening and seeing, reacting to what is actually happening and not to what you have planned to happen or anticipating what you want to happen. And it requires that you are intensively engaged in the content of the situation.

You can be 'present' to the extent that you are so absorbed in the situation that you are not aware of anything else going on. This can be observed in children playing or in lovers being cocooned in their own little world. They are not conscious of what is going on outside the situation in which they are acting. This is part of the other side of the coin of 'being present': you can be 'absent' to parts of the action. You can also be so occupied in the moment that you do not afterwards recall what happened. This often happens to the actors in Dacapo. When we improvise a scene we are so concentrated on making it work in the moment that it can be difficult afterwards to remember the different phases the improvisation went through.

Johnstone tries to define *presence* as a degree or quality of listening, but realizes that it makes no sense to tell people to try to be better listeners. Instead, he says to people, 'Be altered by what's said' (1999: 59). This brings out the relational nature of *presence*. You are present in relation to someone or something, and *presence* is then a quality in your way of reacting to this someone or something. Acting is not about acting but about re-acting – it is not about listening but about being changed by what you hear. This links to Mead's way of explaining communication as a circular movement of gesture–response, where the response gives meaning to the gesture so that you cannot understand the meaning of a gesture in itself, but only in relation to the response (Mead, 1934). Hence I would say that you are *present* when you respond to a gesture spontaneously and are altered by your response. And so, if your response to a gesture does not change you, we will recognize yourself as being less *present*. This points to a paradox in *presence* in that you are recognized as *present* when your identity is shifting, not when it is sustained and unaltered. So, to be less *present* can then be seen as a way of protecting yourself from being altered and risking losing your identity. Trying to stay in control by holding on to what you have planned and arguing for your own ideas rather than listening to others are ways to stay unaltered. And 'knowing who you are' is comforting, while 'being present' may be anxiety-provoking.

I wrote earlier that we have to take seriously the idea that our life is an improvisation, and I will now say that taking it seriously means being 'present' in the improvisation. The risk we are running when we are 'present' is that we will spontaneously change – not only our surroundings, but our own identity in ways we can only know in hindsight. This is of course anxiety-provoking because what we fear is that we may change to someone foolish, someone who is failing, someone stupid. In order to try to avoid this we try to stay in control by repeating actions which have earlier proved successful and which we therefore consider to be 'best practice'.

Improvising in organizations

I began this chapter by describing the Grindy Company's demand to help it implement a planned strategy of implementing corporately chosen values and desired behaviours on the part of the employees. Formulating and implementing strategies, however, constantly bumps up against the day-to-day reality of life in the organization – the hurly-burly of everyday life, as Shotter calls it. Of course organizations must plan. The question is how to deal with the plans in the hurly-burly of everyday life in the organization. Is the plan the final key to all questions arising or is the plan being recreated during every moment with the possibility of being sustained and changed at the same time? What kind of communication is needed in the organization? Basically I see three major ways of viewing communication in change processes.

The first is based on the assumption that you can design and implement a strategy, and when it is implemented it will provide you with the answers you need when in doubt. This is the way the Grindy Company sees communication in a controlled process of change. And it is how I saw my job of teaching improvisations the second year when I believed I could rely on a best practice. This all rests on rational thinking about cause and effect and is based on one-way communication.

The second way is where the employees have been 'empowered' to think for themselves and make some decisions – for instance, in production teams – because the top-down way of communicating has proved inefficient. How to communicate between the different teams then becomes the new challenge. Often this is solved through making rules for good communication within and between the teams. A fast-changing environment may, however, generate an increasing number of rules to a point where it is no longer manageable. In this situation many organizations turn to corporate values as a way of guiding the necessary communication. But even this does not always meet the challenges.

> [R]ule-governed patterns and structures of official social life, clearly exist and are empirically identifiable as such. But . . . the unofficial, everyday hurly-burly of social life is not best thought of as consisting in particular, fixed and empirically identifiable structures and activities. It lacks . . . any fully developed nature at all; it is only partially structured and open, to a certain limited extent, to further development, to further shaping or reshaping by those involved in its conduct.
>
> (Shotter, 2000: 81)

If this is the challenge facing most organizations today, which I believe it is, a third way of understanding communication in organizations is needed. Shotter describes the task in front of us like this: '[O]ur uncertain task is, not only to be human beings, but to be proper and full members of our community, *if only we knew what was entailed in being so*' (Shotter, 2000: 81; emphasis added). To accept this task is not only a question of deciding on a strategy or formulating common rules and values to guide communication. It is an ongoing process of creating meaning between different perspectives, different perceptions of what the decided strategy means in this moment, and what it means to be *a proper and full member of the organizational community.*

Looking at these three ways of seeing communication in organizations, I would say that number one would theatrically be best served by a straightforward performance with the right message. This has never been the work of Dacapo. Number two is how we saw our work from the start in 1995, mapping the reality of the life in an organization and turning it into a performance, which was then shown to the employees. The follow-up work was improvised within the frames of the performance, and the aim of the work was to a large extent to help the audience realize and form ways of improving communication between different parts of the organization. Number three is the challenge we see today. We may still construct small scenes with members of the organization to be performed to other members of the organization. But the process of constructing the scene is already part of the meaning-creating process, and performing it is more a gesture to more meaning-making than presenting a map of some reality. Trying with the participants to make sense of what it means to be a proper and full member of the community in this moment in this situation and what it might take to move forward cannot be rehearsed in advance as a theatre performance. We must be part of the process, yet with a different role from that of other participants. And being part of the process means to be present and hence to improvise.

So, moving away from performances towards more improvising is no coincidence but a logical consequence of how the process of managing organizations and change is developing. We are responding to the needs we experience in the organizations we work with and at the same time we are promoting a way of working we believe is needed. From my experience of being part of an organization in rapid change, and through my experiences of working with clients in many different organizations, it is my conviction that in our daily life in organizations we are faced with the fact that our actions repeatedly turn out to have unexpected meaning as others respond to what we do, not because of some failure in planning or because the strategy was bad, but because this is an essential characteristic of the interaction between interdependent people in a complex organization. One answer to this experience could be better and more careful planning and preparing. Our offer to our clients, however, is of a different kind. We ask people to acknowledge that the work of organizing largely takes place 'live'. It is in the daily interaction among members of the organization that patterns are created and it is in the ongoing gesturing and responding between people on all levels that patterns are being sustained and changed. The work of changing then means paying attention to the fact that we find ourselves, moment by moment, involved in an ongoing improvisation, which demands our presence. And the advantage of using theatre in this work could be understood as expressed by the famous English theatre director Peter Brook: 'If there is a difference between theatre and real life, which may be hard to define, it is always a difference in concentration' (Brook, 1987: 150). Inviting our clients and ourselves to be present in a spontaneous improvisation is what we have come to call 'working live', and it is in this work that improvised theatre, as I have come to understand it, is very useful.

References

Brook, P. (1987) *The Shifting Point*, London: Methuen Drama.
Callery, D. (2001) *Through the Body: A Practical Guide to Physical Theatre*, London: Nick Herns Books.

Ebert, G. and Penka, R. (1985) *Skuespilleren, En grunnbog for skuespilleritdanningen*, Oslo: Gyldendal.

Johnstone, K. (1999) *Impro for Storytellers*, London: Faber and Faber.

Mead, G. H. (1934) *Mind, Self and Society*, Chicago, IL: University of Chicago Press.

Shotter, J. (1993) *Conversational Realities: Constructing Life through Language*, London: Sage.

Shotter, J. (2000) *Real Presences: Meaning as Living Moments in a Participatory World*, Durham: University of New Hampshire.

Spolin, V. (1963) *Improvisation for the Theatre*, Evaston, IL: Northwestern University Press.

Editors' introduction to Chapter 5

In the last three chapters the theme of organizational improvisation was approached from the perspective of theatre and its use in organizational consulting. However, the notion of 'working live' is not restricted to theatre or consulting. It is just as useful in making sense of the activities of managing and leading. In this chapter David Walker takes up the notion in relation to his work as a leader. He explores how as an experienced senior manager in the British health service, he found that no amount of preparation and planning could overcome the need for spontaneous, improvised responses to emerging circumstances. He describes the progress of a new leadership development programme for which he took responsibility and the way he strove to influence how such an activity was conceived and how it was enacted. His own inquiry into what is involved in recognizing himself and being recognized as an effective leader of change affects both the kind of programme he believed would be useful and the way he attempts to legitimize this organizationally in interaction with his peers and other managers.

Leadership is usually thought about in terms of the personal characteristics of leaders and the styles they need to apply, conveying the impression that leaders work with order and clarity. Walker draws attention to a less well-known approach in the literature which emphasizes the 'messiness' and 'sloppiness' of leadership activity, where it is difficult know one's own or others' intentions. Such unpredictability and redundancy require an improvisational approach to leadership. This leads Walker to pick up the themes of spontaneity and risk by elaborating what he suggests is involved in 'leading in the moment'. This requires him to examine what he means conceptually and experientially by the present moment. He turns to his experience as a therapist and to some key writers in the field of therapy to compare concepts of the 'here and now', 'the living present' and 'the moment of meeting'. He focuses our attention on the importance of leading in the moment and on just what this means.

In conducting a leadership programme in a rather novel way for his organization, Walker introduces new practices to others in his organization. He explores how the introduction of new practices arouses anxiety. He argues that this happens because people together develop social defences against the anxieties arising from their work. Many procedures and practices serve this purpose, and so when practices are changed, organizational defence mechanisms are inevitably challenged, and this arouses anxiety. Walker thinks that if leaders are to be able to understand and make sense of rising levels of anxiety, they will be able to live with it and so stay leading in the moment for longer.

5 Leading in the moment: taking risks and living with anxiety

David Walker

In this chapter I explore leading as a process and what it means to 'lead in the moment'. I examine how leading in the moment is a necessary complement to the work of vision and strategy which is also required of leaders and I suggest that too often the anxiety of leading in the moment results in avoiding it. At the time of writing I was a director of a National Health Trust in the United Kingdom and I will explore these themes through my experience of planning and leading an alternative leadership development programme for senior staff in my organization.

I wanted to find a name, a leading idea or title if you like, which would become identified with the programme and give it some identity and coherence. I thought of naming it Janus as a symbol of managers' need to look two ways: upwards or outwards to deal with the imposition of targets, budgets, national standards, patient demands; and inwards or downwards, to manage the demands of their service or teams. However, that name has connotations of two-facedness and untrustworthiness, which was not a good message to convey to participants. Then I stumbled on a half-remembered story of Ariadne. In a previous form she was a goddess of fertility and regeneration, now the daughter of King Minos, who built the labyrinth in ancient Greece. The labyrinth housed the Minotaur, a half-bull, half-man beast which exacted human sacrifices and which was finally slain by Theseus. This was only possible with the help of Ariadne, who gave him the thread which he used to escape from the labyrinth.

Why am I so committed to developing this alternative programme? It is a response to my feeling that I and others are caught up in some overwhelming sacrificial labyrinth of demands and targets and a management discourse within public services which restricts and imprisons rather than enables. Managers stay for short periods of time then move on, or become burned out, either leaving or sinking into cynical uninterest while waiting for their retirement. Clinical staff detach themselves from the need to develop or improve services, concentrating on 'their patients', and do not engage with managers. I was committed to developing a programme within which senior staff could transform their own skills and knowledge by participating in relationships with others, through which they might create new working models for themselves and their teams. I was attempting to create an opportunity for working together, and perhaps through this a thread might emerge which could enable them to slay their own Minotaurs and escape their own labyrinths. In introducing this programme I was inspired by a similar programme developed by a colleague in another NHS Trust (Sarra, 2005).

In what follows I track the development of Ariadne from the exploratory session with staff, through the process of writing a proposal for the board, to forming a steering group, bringing together a staff/facilitator group, gaining research money from the NHS national leadership centre, the first meeting of facilitators, the first two days of the programme and the days after this. Throughout, I use these stages of development not to understand the movement of a programme over time and the different emphasis required at each stage, although clearly these are important factors, but to illustrate aspects of leadership in the moment. I am concerned with how, in my role as director responsible, I am able to participate in the process of improvisational leadership required for Ariadne to emerge. I am attempting to monitor and understand something of my own and others' anxieties in relation to this process.

Through exploring my experience in the moment, I will investigate the process of developing and working with leadership and followership in a way which attempts to take account of the complexities and messiness of leading in organizational life. There is a large literature which tries to identify what leadership is and what makes successful leaders. Much of this work has identified the characteristics of leaders and the styles needed to be applied in different situations (e.g. Fiedler, 1967; Bales, 1970; Hersey and Blanchard, 1988). This literature suggests that the leader can sit outside the organization as an autonomous individual and apply strategies to move it forward. One such strategy is the development of competency-based frameworks, which implies that there are definite and certain truths about leadership that can be learned and applied. Mainstream authors such as Kotter (1982) and Davis *et al.* (1992) write about leadership as though the leader works with order and clarity. However, there are authors who have drawn attention to the disorderly nature of leadership roles. For example, Binney *et al.* (2003) talk about the 'messiness' of leadership, and Stern (2004) has a similar idea in relation to the psychotherapist's work when he writes of the relevance and importance of 'sloppiness'. By messiness, Binney *et al.* refer to the lack of clarity in organizational life, including complex interrelationships, conflicting tasks and ever-changing environments. There is no order waiting to be uncovered for which a diagnostic prescription can be given. Stern's term 'sloppiness' is related but slightly different. He refers to processes of interaction which occur between two people as they attempt to communicate and move forward together. He suggests that sloppiness has several characteristics, including 'intentional fuzziness', defined as the difficulty of knowing your own or others' intentions; unpredictability; redundancy; and improvisation. He suggests that these characteristics of sloppiness have usually been perceived as unhelpful aspects of communication to be eliminated. Instead, he suggests that these are essential aspects of a process which allows 'unlimited creativity' to occur (Stern, 2004: 158).

Both terms, messiness and sloppiness, reflect the reality of the leader's experience, and it is important to pay attention to this disorderly experience which can create anxiety. How do those in leadership roles survive the ongoing complex processes of leading and following within which this disorder exists, and where does one pay attention? What leadership processes honour complexity and the reality of the experience, opening this up rather than closing down in some prescriptive manner? I think this was experienced in the first meeting to plan the development of Ariadne.

Planning the development of Ariadne

It was a Wednesday morning and seventy senior staff of the organization were attending a morning event held in the hospitality suite of our local premiership football team. Each year for four half-days, these 'top' seventy staff met together to discuss matters of relevance for the Trust or to hear presentations from the chief executive, chairman or others concerning NHS policy matters. The purpose was to build corporate identity and vision in the Trust, but often these events were badly planned since the executive left planning until the last moment. I had been suggesting for some time that we could plan a series of integrated staff development days and should expand these, as well as do something different with the time. The chief executive had agreed with me and asked me to lead a discussion to explore a new approach. I was given an hour and a half for this.

During the coffee break, I realized that my time had already been reduced as a result of the previous session overrunning. This last session had been a rather dull presentation by two executives about the latest national requirement as part of the NHS modernization agenda. Energy in the session was low and participants were reluctant to return from their coffee break. I was feeling nervous as to whether I would be able to capture people's attention, aware that I was introducing a different way of thinking, but also feeling a little irritated by the previous speakers stealing my time. I wondered if there was some unspoken rivalry within the executive which was blocking my contribution.

Simon (the chief executive) talked to me about his anxiety that the previous session had fallen flat. I enlisted his help and that of another director to herd people back into the room. I was determined not to let the restriction in time alter my approach, which I had planned in order that, after a few introductory remarks from me and some scene-setting, the participants would have time to talk with each other. So, I think I was having to deal with the messiness of everyday life in organizations as many come together with conflicting agendas and competing tasks, as well as work with the 'sloppiness' of relationships.

I had prepared some introductory thoughts, introducing simple ideas from complexity and collaborative inquiry work to illustrate my way of thinking. I wanted to begin a discussion out of which some commitment to a development programme might arise and which would stimulate senior staff to think afresh together. As I spoke, I was aware of people in the audience responding to me and nodding in agreement. There was interest and a sense of connection in the room. During this brief introductory talk I said:

> 'Complexity theory suggests that change occurs through the interaction of diverse agents. Change cannot be predicted or determined, so having an approach relying solely on strategy and target-setting will not work. With a mix of difference (diversity), connections between people, energy or information and ongoing interaction between people, change will occur. Too much of these ingredients may cause mayhem, too little will cause stuckness. This suggests that change is more likely to occur through developing conversations between people and supporting this process. It suggests that a multi-voiced approach providing space and opportunity for staff to reflect and make their own choices about action is more likely to lead to real and lasting change of relevance than a top-down target-driven strategy.'

I also mentioned how work by Kennedy and Griffiths (2003) highlighted another supporting factor for this approach. They developed a collaborative approach in mental health teams which showed that when teams were allowed and supported to develop their own local solutions to problems, change occurred more easily and morale improved. Then I said:

> 'The top-down control often seen in the NHS inhibits staff taking initiative and developing innovative practice. So, part of my agenda is how we develop a programme together which will make use of some of these approaches and harness energy and creativity in our staff. Our task today is to begin this exploration and identify what development needs you have and also what the issues in your services are which you would like to address through such a programme.'

I set the group two tasks: first, in pairs, to discuss what they would like to gain from a programme personally, professionally and for their service; second, in small groups, to brainstorm what the main issues of concern for their service were, which they would like to address and resolve through joint working on such a development programme. The room started to buzz, energy levels rose, and all engaged with interest and enthusiasm in the task, many commenting that they were encouraged by this new emphasis. I think these discussions were working with what Stern has termed sloppiness; that is, the conversations were not predetermined and planned but involved intentional fuzziness, unpredictability, redundancy and improvisation out of which some novel movement could occur. So, Ariadne had begun to develop.

It is important, though, to point out that 'sloppiness' is the prerogative of thoughtful and skilled leaders/psychotherapists, not an excuse for lack of rigour in practice or theory. Stern makes the point that 'sloppiness is potentially creative only when it occurs within a well-established framework' (2004: 164). I suggest that the ability to see and manage the confusions of everyday life, which occur in organizations and are manifestations of the relationships as well as the 'external' events, is crucial. Working within this reality rather than avoiding it is an essential aspect of leadership.

Complexities of leading and following

Complexity theory may suggest that all I can do is enter with my intentions into interactions with others with their intentions, out of which something new will be created under no one individual's control. This is what I was attempting to do in the senior staff introductory session just described.

I think it is important to reflect for a moment about intentions. If complexity theory suggests that the future is under perpetual construction and that the past is continually reconstructed in relation to the present moment, then we cannot determine what happens or choose it. This does not mean, however, that there is no personal choice or freedom; we can have intentions and indeed need to be clear and purposeful about our intentions in relation to others. Stern (2004) draws on the literature to show how important the world of intentions is. He posits that there is an intersubjective motivation, as distinct from an attachment motivation or an instinctual motivation. He suggests that the ability to read the intentions of others develops at an early age and is a crucial part of developing the intersubjective field. He draws on research evidence which has shown that even very young infants have the ability to recognize and relate to the intentions of others. He writes:

> We see the human world in terms of intentions. And we act in terms of our own. You cannot function with other humans without reading or inferring their motives or intentions. This reading or attributing of intentions is our primary guide to responding and initiating action. Inferring intentions in human behavior appears to be universal. It is a

mental primitive. It is how we parse and interpret our human
surroundings.

(Stern, 2004: 86–87)

So, the intersubjective motivations of leaders and followers are crucial,
particularly in terms of how each is able to recognize and respond to the
others' intentions and also in terms of how shared intentions are
developed. Griffin highlights how people are 'forming intentions on the
basis of the cult values they have from their past' (2002: 189). By cult
values he means, drawing from the work of Mead, those values which set
up idealized ends that cannot be achieved and can divert from everyday
practice. As these cult values are functionalized – that is, as the
ideas/beliefs/ideals are translated into everyday practice – the different
intentions of each individual interact and conflict in the living present and
something will emerge, and change will occur or not. This process can
clearly be seen in the workings of any multidisciplinary team as its
members struggle to achieve interdisciplinary working.

There is also a tendency, often reinforced by followers, to wish for
leadership which will produce answers and meet the desire for the
removal of discomfort. I am challenging this myth of expertise and
exploring the process which takes place as leaders try to establish an
alternative mode of legitimizing activity and how this form of authority
may be recognized.

First steering group meeting

It is four months after the exploratory session with senior staff, and
things have moved on apace. I have presented a paper to the Trust board
and been given some funding and full board support to proceed. I have
designed a structure for the programme and we have set up a steering
group to take this forward. 'What are the outcomes we wish for and how
will you measure them?', asks our newly joined Director of Nursing.
My heart sinks at the question. Then James, the Director of Forensic
Services, says:

> 'If I am going to send my staff on this and take them out of the
> service for a large amount of time I need to know what they will
> learn. Couldn't you run a modular programme and staff could only
> sign up to learn particular modules and skills in areas they were
> deficient in?'

My heart sinks further. I thought we had thrashed all this through at the Trust board and the executive team meetings, and that people understood the concept I was taking forward. I feel disappointed and angry that members of the steering group appear to be questioning the approach and feel like withdrawing and not bothering to reply. I stutter a couple of half-replies and people continue to chip in with 'bright ideas', making me feel we are talking different languages.

This brief interaction shows how there is still tension between the different discourses in the executive team. Broadly, the difference is between a 'traditional' approach, which believes that knowledge and leadership skills are either permanent traits which are inborn or competencies which can be identified and taught to individuals, and the approach I am trying to take forward, which suggests that leadership and knowledge emerge in the present moment as people make sense together of the complex demands facing them. Of course, these contrasting underlying assumptions, based on alternative theoretical formulations of both person and how novelty occurs, lead to markedly different forms of programme.

I am aware of challenging other directors' beliefs and value systems as well as my own; my withdrawal is partly a response to this and a need to gather my wits. In retrospect, it might have been possible to open up a debate about this and discuss together the underlying theoretical assumptions which were behind our positions. This staying in the 'present moment' might have allowed a novel process of relating to emerge between us, or might have been too confusing for us to participate in. Somehow I was unable to do this, though I will return to talk about what made this difficult in a moment.

First I will explain the background to this meeting. After acceptance of my proposal for Ariadne by the Trust board, there was enthusiasm from my co-directors and endorsement from the chief executive for me to lead the programme. I asked for volunteers to join the steering group. Surprisingly, nearly all the executive team members wished to join, so we agreed together which directors would be members and that I would invite a non-executive director and our new manager of service modernization. I felt confirmed by the executive in this leadership role and so was surprised to encounter some resistance at the first steering group. On reflection, I realized this came from the two executive members who had remained quiet in our previous discussions, and two new members.

I wish to reflect a little on what was happening in this first steering group meeting. I think I was hoping for a different sort of meeting to take place but had not properly prepared. I am learning of the need to be prepared and then forget the preparation in order to allow something new to emerge; both are necessary. Many meetings occur in organizational life as ritual, routine or defensive manoeuvres. I had decided not to run a traditional meeting with agenda and minutes, hoping that a different form of participative conversation would take place.

However, I may have misjudged the degree of rivalry and anxiety about the new approach which I was introducing. I was making a bid for leadership within the executive, and some of the difficulty in the first meeting had to do with our negotiation of power and form of discourse. In this context, I think I was ambivalent about taking strong leadership within my peer group, as well as hoping for a more collaborative approach. It is important to note that the two directors voicing most doubts had not been part of the executive team's previous discussion. I think their questioning and my uncertainty fed each other and contributed to our developing a discussion which lacked focus and felt something of a struggle.

On reflection, after the meeting, I realized that people were looking for stronger leadership from me, and my wish to gain ideas from them had disempowered me from giving this. At the second steering group I was much clearer about what the structure and plan were, and what I needed from the steering group members, which led to a more fruitful collaborative meeting. In a sense I took control of the meeting, not out of anxiety but out of recognition that I had the knowledge and skills necessary to understand and explain what we were attempting to develop, using my authority appropriately. However, I think I needed to go through this process to recognize what was needed by the others and to test out my own doubts and reservations about, and confidence in, the new approach I was taking forward. Perhaps it was only through the rigorous questioning and testing of my ideas by the two doubting directors that it became possible for me and others to see the merits of what we were trying to take forward.

So, I was involved in an emerging process of leadership and followership in relation to Ariadne. Of course, this process had been taking place within the executive for many years as our working relationships negotiate power and distance and dominant discourses. In relation to the steering group it is interesting to note how the second meeting felt very different and was 'successful' after the struggles of the first meeting.

I have used this narrative partly to illustrate the emergence of a leadership process within a group of peers and something of the anxieties about rivalry and authority involved in this process of negotiation. It also highlights the difficulty in the face of such intersubjective pressures of leading in the moment. Another of the difficulties of leading in the moment is to maintain the ability to live with incompleteness, allowing movement and flow to occur, rather than searching for closure, especially when others want certainty.

Leadership in the moment

What do I mean by 'leadership in the moment'? I mean paying attention to where I am now and what is occurring in my own mind, if you like, taking my experience seriously, allowing for a thinking and feeling self in the presence of others through listening to my bodily responses, physical, cognitive and emotional, and being reflexive and subjective when in a leadership role. As I write about leadership in the moment I am aware of the importance of the ability to be fully present and the quality of presence a leader is able to bring. It seems to me that a leader present, in the moment, responding spontaneously enables others to feel good enough to also participate spontaneously. There is something about the connection established between leaders and followers which is important for movement and healthy organizational functioning. I will use a story to illustrate further some of what I mean.

The live interview

'My section really enjoyed the department day we had,' says Maggie. 'They were particularly impressed by your interview and had respect for you and the areas you cover.' I felt pleased with this feedback, which concerned a psychology department training day some three months earlier. I had organized this day to help us think together about our work in teams and the organization, and enlisted the help of a theatre company. As part of the day I was interviewed in front of some seventy members of the department as a way for department members to hear and feel more of 'me'. It is not possible to do the interview justice in this chapter but I wish to use a small excerpt from midway through the interview to illustrate being present in a way which allows for a different contact between leaders and followers.

'What were your reflections about the play we have worked with today?'
Immediately a flippant thought springs into my head. 'Oh god, I can't say
that!', I think. My mind is blank as I struggle to retrieve something more
erudite to say. Realizing this, I say:

> 'Well, maybe I shouldn't say this but it is the only thing in my head
> just now and unless I say it I won't be able to say anything else. What
> I first thought when you asked the question was "What a load of
> rubbish psychologists talk sometimes." That was my first reflection on
> the play just now.'

I continue that the play reflected well many of the situations in which
psychologists find themselves. I draw similarities between the clinical
team we have just seen portrayed and the executive team I work in,
commenting on power, control and rivalry.

> 'I am realizing all I can do is think about how I respond in the
> immediate situation and worry less about planning and where we are
> trying to get to, or indeed how to change the other person. Increasingly
> I realize all I can do is risk a response and worry less about being in
> control.'

Being interviewed in this manner was an important open act of leadership
which altered the balance of power relations in the department. I think
that through this interview I was exploring a different way of legitimizing
activity, using authority and exerting leadership. Obviously it is important
to be clear about function, hierarchy, roles, and degrees of technical
knowledge and experiential wisdom. Also important are the appropriate
meeting structures to enable the transmission of the organization's goals
and purposes. Clearly, these are the responsibility of the leadership.
However, this is not enough. Leadership is also the process of entering
into lively relationship with others. The interview was a live narrative of
my leadership approach and an example of leadership in action, the
conversational structure of which allowed for openness and self-
disclosure, giving information in an easily digestible
personal/professional way. In a sense it allowed me to be present as leader
without worrying about being liked or getting it right. It was not
rehearsed, so all my attention was in staying 'live'.

In this chapter, I am arguing that for leadership to be effective, two
aspects have to be taken account of: leadership as a process which occurs
between people; and leadership as occurring in the present moment.
I expand on these themes in the following sections.

Leadership as process

From a complex responsive processes perspective, individuals form and are formed by groups at the same time. Themes of leadership and authority are created simultaneously between leaders and followers. It follows that leadership is a process which occurs between people rather than being simply to do with individual characteristics of leaders. Griffin (2002) develops the idea of leadership themes emerging out of the ongoing interaction between leaders and followers in the living present in which there is always the potential for emergent novelty. I think this notion of leadership as a process is crucial and provides a perspective that is fundamentally different from mainstream views. I am distinguishing the appointment of leaders in roles from the process of interaction which occurs between people in which leadership themes emerge and real change in organizations occurs. As Griffin (2002: 206–207) explains, a systemic self-organization perspective relies on a linear notion of time so that the future can be split off and planned for by leaders. From the perspective of participative self-organization (complex responsive processes), the past and future are continuously being recreated in present interactions.

Binney *et al.* (2003), when discussing the tasks of leadership and the variety of models of leadership, say, 'The real work of leadership is in leaving the models behind and discovering in the here and now, with this group of people, this organization and in this context, what leadership is possible and needed.' This raises two issues for me. First, leadership occurs in a context and is not something which can be learned and applied. Second, it raises questions as to what the individual in the leadership role brings to the task.

Traditional approaches to leadership training involve teaching skills and competencies. I question whether this is a useful approach, because leadership is not a 'state' or a set of skills an individual possesses to be learned and applied, but a continuous process which occurs in relation with and to others. However, clearly some individuals are better leaders than others are, so what is it that makes them so? Perhaps it is more fruitful to speak of potential rather than skill, the former containing a sense of movement as opposed to the latter, which gives a static sense of skill. Skill suggests something that exists and is permanent rather than dependent on context and relationship. I suggest that some individuals, owing to a life history which emerges in processes of relating, have greater potential, which then emerges in the context of the leadership–followership relations.

So, I am interested in how one leads in the moment and in the processes in which leadership actions occur. By bringing together a diverse group of eight facilitators, a participative researcher and an external consultant, I am exerting individual leadership of Ariadne through creating a leadership team in which my leadership is emerging in their recognition. I am recognizing that leadership of the programme is a process in which we all participate and which is created between us. This is different from the perspective of some leadership writers (e.g. Bales, 1970), who suggest that leadership can be broken down into different tasks and these tasks undertaken by different people. Here I am suggesting that leadership and followership themes emerge out of the interactions between people and that it is important to pay attention to this process. Between us a way forward will emerge and different leadership acts will be taken according to the role each is in. But what does it mean to lead in the moment?

Present moment

Much of leadership is by necessity connected to past events – for example, when investigating a complaint or a crisis which has occurred in a healthcare setting. It is also connected to the future; for example, predicting political agendas, staffing patterns or changes in healthcare trends may be important requirements for future success and survival. One's view of time is thus important as far as understanding leadership is concerned. Most of the leadership literature is based on a linear notion of time in which the future is predictable from the past and the present is only a moment on the way to the future from the past.

The perspective of complex responsive processes, however, takes a different view of time, namely that of the living present, a concept drawn from the work of Mead. Mead (1932) explored the relationship between past, present and future in a collection of lectures published posthumously under the title *The Philosophy of the Present*. In one of these, 'The Present as the Locus of Reality', he examines what the present consists of: 'the present is a passage constituted by processes whose earlier phases determine in certain respects their later phase. Reality then is always in a present' (Mead, 1932: 57). He suggests that the past does not exist in its own right, although of course actual events have taken place, but only in how it is remembered, re-experienced and reinterpreted in the present. The present then becomes the moment in which the emergent appears, informed from the past and leading to the future. This means that 'the past, which must then be looked at from the standpoint of the emergent, becomes a different past' (ibid.: 36). I think this leads to the notion that within the present moment the past reappears and is transformed and leads to an emerging future. However, the only reality is in the present moment.

> A present then, as contrasted with the abstraction of mere passage, is not a piece cut out anywhere from the temporal dimension of uniformly passing reality. Its chief reference is to the emergent event, that is, to the occurrence of something which is more than the processes which have led up to it and which by its change, continuance or disappearance, adds to later passages a content they would not otherwise have possessed.
>
> (ibid.: 52)

This notion gives primacy to the present as the moment in which meaning and transformation continually occur, being continually re-formed in the present moment. The significance of the future is that it gives meaning as anticipation in the present. In a later lecture, 'Emergence and Identity', Mead again emphasizes the emergent, transformative quality of the present:

> All of the past is in the present as the conditioning nature of passage, and all the future arises out of the present as the unique events that transpire. To unravel this existent past in the present and on the basis of it to previse the future is the task of science.
>
> (ibid.: 62)

Shaw explains the term 'living present' further:

> This is similar to what I mean by thinking from within the movement of our participation, a movement into a paradoxical known–unknown. This social process of learning our way forward is paradoxical because the past (our personally experienced histories of social relating) help us to recognize the future and give it meaning, yet the future is also changing the meaning of the very past with which we can recognize the future. This occurs in the movement of our experience in a present that we can no longer think of as a dimensionless dot in a linear flow of time, but a present we could think of as having its own fractal time structure, in other words self similar at all scales. In this series we have coined the term *living present* to describe such a lived in experience of presentness, to open up for serious consideration how conversation as communicative

action in the living present is transformational of personal and social realities, of the patterning of identity and difference.

(2002: 46)

Group analysis also develops the importance of 'here and now'. Foulkes and Anthony write, 'Group analytic psychotherapy emphasizes *the immediate present* in the therapeutic transactions (the "*here and now*") and has a more direct effect on the patient's current life situation and his behavior' ([1957] 1975: 41; emphasis added). In discussing leadership in group analysis, Pines (1983) comments that the analyst 'emphasizes the "here and now" aspect of the (group) situation'. Stacey makes clear the difference between the 'here and now' of psychotherapy and the 'living present' of complex responsive processes. He suggests the 'here and now' is distinguished from the 'there and then', and focusing on 'here and now' means looking only at the emotional relationships occurring in the room at a given time. From this perspective he suggests that intellectual conversation and focusing on relationships outside the room are seen as defensive moves. He says:

> This is a linear view of time in which the present of the 'here and now' is a point separating the past from the future. The living present, on the other hand, is a circular notion of time in which expectations forming in the present about the future affect the iteration of the past that is forming the expectation of the future.
>
> (2003: 146)

What I believe complex responsive process theory is saying in relation to leaders participating in organizations is very similar to what Stern is saying in relation to psychotherapists working with patients. Both are saying that important change develops out of the connections which emerge in the moment-to-moment interactions between people, and therefore that paying attention to that moment is crucial. However, this present moment contains within it both past experience and meaning, and future direction. It is during this 'now' moment that past events are recalled and re-experienced, perhaps resulting in a different understanding and recreating of the past. At the same time it is in this 'now' moment that intentions form and are re-formed by a future which emerges moment by moment but which does not pre-exist.

Stern (2004), together with his colleagues in the Boston Study Group, develops the importance of intersubjectivity in relation to the present moment, which is the moment when two or more people create and develop meaningful experience together. He suggests that intersubjective motivation is crucial and distinguishes this from both attachment motivation and instinctual motivation. Although he is developing his thought in the context of psychotherapeutic work, I think it is very useful to apply to the work of leaders in organizations also. His views link with those of Mead, and his detailed investigation of the 'present moment' helps to understand further the notion of 'living present'. He describes the 'present moment', the 'moment of meeting' and the 'now moment'. These are implicit aspects of the relationship between psychotherapist and patient, and he suggests that they are not usually attended to. He is not advocating ignoring interpretation or the paying of attention to facts or events in past experience, but suggesting complementing this with a focus on 'presentness'. This is similar to my suggesting that it is important for leaders to complement the work on strategy, vision and foresight with an attention to the relationships and emotions occurring in the moment. By 'present moment' Stern is referring to 'the span of time in which psychological processes group together very small units of perception into the smallest global unit (a gestalt) that has a sense or meaning in the context of a relationship' (2004: 245). He suggests that small moments of time of between one and ten seconds are subjectively experienced as an uninterrupted now. Each present moment potentially contains a lived story. When there is a connection between two persons there is a mutually created moment which is meaningful and mutative. He refers to the 'present moment' as having psychological work to do as it somehow 'chunk[s] and make[s] sense of the moment as it is passing, not afterwards' (ibid.: xv). Because of this, he draws on the Greek word *Kairos* as a subjective and psychological unit of time which records the moment of something coming into being.

He describes a 'now moment' as a 'present moment' which 'suddenly arises in a session as an emergent property of the moving along process' (ibid.: 245). This 'now moment' challenges the existing form, suggesting that a new state may come into being which raises anxieties. 'A now moment is so called because there is an immediate sense that the existing intersubjective field is threatened, that an important change in the relationship is possible' (ibid.: 167).

One way out of the tension of this 'now moment' may be a 'moment of meeting'. By this Stern is referring to a present moment between two participants which potentially resolves the crisis created by a now moment. It thereby reshapes the intersubjective field and alters the relationship. It is called forth as an emergent property from the micro-context of the now moment and must be exquisitely sensitive to this context.

(ibid.: 244)

Stern emphasizes the importance of intersubjective consciousness in present moments, when both participants share and co-create a lived experience during which there is overlapping and co-creating of consciousness. The desire for intersubjective contact drives the moving-along process in the therapy relationship. He argues that this contains three intersubjective aspects: orienting, when patient and therapist test out where each other is; sharing experience and being known through enlarging the intersubjective field or mental territory held in common; and defining and redefining of oneself using reflection from the other.

So, if a moment of meeting within the intersubjective field is crucial for novelty and movement to occur, something other to emerge, then an authentic spontaneous response is necessary from the therapist in the present moment. Theory and the application of technique alone are not enough. The arrival of a now moment requires something from the therapist other than a technically competent response if a moment of meeting is to emerge. If there is a successful moment of meeting, the intersubjective field is expanded and further movement is possible. It can be difficult for the therapist to stay with this process as anxiety levels increase.

Burch (2004) explores the relevance of closeness and intimacy between patient and therapist. He writes about 'something missing' in analytic therapy and the importance of the real here-and-now intersubjective relationship, which involves conscious and unconscious connections, out of which a new way of being may emerge. He suggests that the moment of meeting described by Stern and colleagues is similar to 'ego to ego' meeting. He equates this to 'positive contact between patient and therapist which is experienced in closeness and intimacy' (ibid.: 367), suggesting that closeness is conscious contact and intimacy arises out of unconscious connection. If this is so, then anxiety will be aroused within the therapist as to how to negotiate his or her way through the necessary intersubjective field of intimacy and closeness without violating important boundaries for the patient, or indeed the therapist.

Now I think this way of understanding the present and the intersubjective context within which the therapist has to act and pay attention to the implicit rather than the explicit context has important implications for leadership in organizations. Stern has begun to identify a way to open up and understand the present which has implications for practice both for psychotherapists and for leaders. I think Stern is moving away from a more traditional psychoanalytic approach which suggests that the past is replayed in the present, and nearing a complex responsive processes perspective of the living present and the circular notion of time.

> A key challenge, therefore, for leaders and the people around them, was somehow to hang on to their dreams while engaging with the here and now. Paradoxically, the focus on setting vision and direction – intended to instil a positive, forward looking mentality – could leave people compliant, resentful and paralysed. It was by beginning to name uncomfortable parts of current reality that energy was released and people could look forward. This tension was truly at the heart of leadership transition: the more leaders could live intensely, in the moment, and let go of the anxiety to impose themselves on events, the more effective they could be in leading change.
>
> (Binney *et al.*, 2003: 77)

I am reminded of an incident that occurred during the second day of Ariadne which I think can be understood as a moment of meeting.

Ariadne day 2: the challenge leading to a moment of meeting

'You are changing the rules. Why shouldn't we form larger and smaller groups if we want?', challenges John. This seems a reasonable question and I feel stuck for an answer.

In Stern's terms, I think this can be seen as a 'now moment', which I will call 'now moment one'. As the programme has progressed over the previous two days, various key moments have arisen which have led to a deepening or lessening of the relationships between participants and facilitators. When these moments occur I think they can be recognized and experienced at the time. This is similar to the moving-along process of therapy. For a few seconds after John asked his question, he and I share eye contact and there is a process occurring between us of which we are both aware and which can be observed by the whole group. This has the properties which Stern ascribes to the 'now moment'. The emotional tension in the room has risen, John and I have entered into an affectively charged moment which could alter our relationship, and I believe we are both aware of this and experience a sense of being at risk. This moment also presents a challenge to the rules and existing framework of the programme, which means everyone is to a greater or lesser extent at risk. My anxiety increases, as I believe John's does as he mounts the challenge, and the sixty or so others in the room wait as an anticipating audience. We are all very much engaged in the present moment.

Having asked the participants to form into learning sets of six, we are now wondering how to manage a situation where we have one group of three, and several much larger than six. Does it matter? What is happening here? I find myself wondering what to do. Is this a rebellion which needs resisting? Is it a creative solution which is emerging? One of the other facilitators is struggling to manage the situation and I feel that as 'leader' of the programme I need to intervene. I repeat: 'The task was to form into groups of six.' I have no idea how to shift this, or where the discussion will lead, but feel I need to hang on to our original task. I see this as an attempt by me to assert the status quo and keep the arrangements as they were; if you like, I am unable to take the plunge into unknown territory and am resorting to technique and safe ground. This could be seen as taking a perspective informed from group analytic thought in which it is my task to maintain the boundary and the structure agreed in advance. This does not, however, lead to a moment of meeting which would enable a new direction to emerge and a deepening of rapport and intersubjective contact.

Another takes up the challenge: 'You say this is a course we create ourselves but then when we do something you do not want . . . you do not allow it to happen. Why can't we have groups the size we want?' (now moment 2). This can be understood as a re-emergence of the now moment with an increase in affect so that anxiety rises. I feel I have to move into new territory.

'If this really is the most appropriate arrangement, then fine, but I am concerned that by staying in these sizes we are avoiding tackling something else,' I reply. Then John says:

> 'We do this all the time at work to the staff we manage. We tell them to do things which do not seem a big deal to us but maybe it really affects them. This is how the staff must feel when asked to do something by us.'

John has just made an important link for himself and the others between the process occurring here and now and the daily work of leading/managing others.

I think this is akin to the moment of meeting. Between us we had created a response to the crisis through participating together in the present which was sensitive and appropriate to the issues at stake. The participants were able to return to the task and go about the business of re-forming into groups of six. It is through these moment-by-moment interactions and encounters that leaders and followers, together, co-create them. I think Stern's work helps us to understand this process further and enables a theoretical understanding of the present which has practical implications. One automatically changes practice as the focus of attention is altered.

Ariadne leaves Minos

I have just completed running the first two days of the first Ariadne programme with a staff team of ten and a cohort of fifty-two participants, all senior staff in my organization. I am replaying conversations which occurred, imagining new ones and new movements, thinking of the next days and future plans, wondering how the days were received, sensing excitement and some anxiety about the novelty of the approach as well as turning over in my mind a 'real' problem which needs solving, namely how to tackle a difficult and obstructive small clique of three which has formed – how much to negotiate and how much to tell them. So this too is the process of leadership, the ongoing conversations with oneself, as the past is re-experienced and used to inform the next part of the process.

This process continued three days later when I discussed the first two days with the executive team. There is some anxiety and doubt about the programme. I am aware of how new this approach is to executive colleagues and some of those on the programme. There is some uneasiness and doubt about where we are going. Again I am asked about outcomes, and what the learning sets will produce. I find myself becoming anxious and feeling a little threatened, wondering how much I need to shift the emphasis of the programme. I try to remain consistent and say I would be worried if the approach had not unsettled people a little. Learning is unsettling, but the majority of participants were engaged and involved throughout.

Later the chief executive assures me privately that he still supports the programme but says some of the executive colleagues are worried that we have adopted such a high-risk strategy. 'Let me say first that I am one hundred per cent behind the programme but I think I need to say something of what the directors are concerned about,' says the chief executive, Simon. 'Fine, let's be open,' I reply. He continues, 'Some of the directors didn't say it in the meeting but they are concerned about unsettling the staff. They think we have a good organizational culture here and that the programme is in danger of destroying that.'

We continue to talk together about the first two days of Ariadne, which had taken place the previous week. I comment that if staff had not been unsettled, a little anxious and reacting to the programme, we would have not done anything useful. I remind him that we have good staff and that the intention of the programme was always to bring in a different approach to leadership in the organization. However, that night at home I find myself feeling unsettled and restless. I am reminded of two telephone conversations with one of the Ariadne facilitators (Hazel, a fellow director, wished to be included as a staff member on the programme). After the end of the two days I had to help her think through some issues in relationship to her learning set since she was feeling very anxious. I thought little of that until listening to my answerphone two evenings later. 'I spoke to Simon today and he is very anxious. I think you need to speak to him soon,' was the gist of the message from her. I did nothing since I was about to go away for the weekend, and my meeting with Simon occurred some three days later.

Understanding anxiety

So there is much anxiety around in the organization about Ariadne. How can this be understood? I think if leaders are to be able to work differently and manage their own anxiety in relation to the anxiety of others, it is important to have some way of understanding and making sense of this. I believe this understanding enables the anxiety to be lived with or a decision made as to whether the anxiety is a sign that something is amiss and needs attending to. It is necessary to think about when this anxiety is healthy and when it is unhealthy. I will briefly draw on, first, a psychoanalytic perspective, then an intersubjective perspective and finally a complex response processes perspective to illuminate and understand something of the anxiety aroused by Ariadne in myself and others.

Menzies Lyth (1959, 1988) writes about 'socially constructed defence mechanisms' that occur in organizations and their interrelationship to individual defence mechanisms. She draws on the work of Melanie Klein, which identifies anxiety and defence mechanisms as crucial to the development and functioning of the personality. Menzies Lyth applies these ideas to human organizations. She suggests that social structures are developed to meet individual psychic emotional need. Socially constructed defence mechanisms form in organizations to defend the individuals against the anxiety inherent in the work. At first, the individuals externalize their individual defence mechanisms and then, over time, they coalesce to form socially constructed defence mechanisms. These then become externalized into various practices, rituals and routines which become embedded in the life of the organization and which serve a defensive purpose that may be at odds with the primary task of the organization. As new individuals join the organization, their own internal psychic defence mechanisms, designed to manage inherent anxiety, will be confronted by the socially constructed defence mechanisms within the organization which are embodied in practice. Individuals whose individual defence mechanisms resonate with those of the organization are more likely to survive and prosper, while others may find life less comfortable.

The introduction of new practices or ideas within an organization will challenge organizational defences, which in turn will challenge individual defence mechanisms. I think this is one way to understand the anxious reaction to Ariadne, which was put into words by the director who said, 'This is a high-risk strategy . . . we have a good organizational culture here, and we are worried you may disrupt it.'

However, without challenge to, or modification of, the defence mechanisms, change and movement cannot take place. The question may be how much modification of the defence mechanisms is needed and how much anxiety can be tolerated. 'The characteristic feature of the social defence system . . . is its orientation to helping the individual avoid the experience of anxiety, guilt, doubt and uncertainty' (Menzies Lyth, 1988: 63). She suggests that underlying anxiety is inherent in all individuals, and the avoidance of experiencing this primitive anxiety drives the development of social defence structures. 'Little attempt is made positively to help the individual confront the anxiety-evoking experiences and, by so doing, to develop her capacity to tolerate and deal more effectively with the anxiety' (ibid.: 63).

So, from this perspective anxiety is aroused in individuals by Ariadne because the challenge to the organization's defence mechanisms is deeply upsetting for the individuals within it, as the harmony between individual and organizational defence mechanisms is challenged. I think the programme is trying to face and address the real anxiety inherent in the work rather than avoid it, which, of course, is disturbing.

How can this experience of anxiety be understood by drawing on Stern's work? Stern's work is based on a different theoretical understanding of anxiety and change. His is based not on a model which assumes inherent qualities and deficits against which defences have to be employed, but on one which emphasizes the creating of 'contexts in which new emergent properties are permitted and encouraged to arise' (Stern, 2004: 179).

From this perspective, anxiety will arise out of the intersubjective relationships within the present moment rather than be an internal state dependent on defence mechanisms. Stern proposes 'intersubjective anxiety' similar to an existential anxiety. He suggests that this arises in the context of the intersubjective relationship when the orientation process does not 'provide sufficiently clear coordinates about where one is in the intersubjective field' (ibid.: 243).

So, the anxiety aroused through Ariadne could be understood as arising from many present moments which have the capacity to move through now moments into moments of meeting. This relies on our being able to talk together in novel ways which then unsettle but broaden the intersubjective context of the executive team or that between Simon and myself.

> One of the obstacles in shaping a spontaneous and authentic response to fulfill a moment of meeting is the anxiety experienced by the therapist during the now moment. The easiest and fastest way to reduce anxiety is to fall back on, and hide behind standard technical moves. Both the anxiety and the sense of being disarmed are eliminated, but the therapy may have lost the opportunity to leap ahead.
>
> (ibid.: 169)

I think this is a helpful way to understand the reactions to Ariadne. During our meeting reviewing the first two days, Simon expressed concern that I was not in charge enough in the large group meetings, allowing others to talk too much. On the contrary, I felt I was able to allow the large group discussion to flow and did not need to impose myself. He had wanted to give a PowerPoint presentation to the group and I had asked him not to, but instead to introduce a few points and then engage in conversation. Trying to get me to resort to traditional techniques for leadership and presentation, I think, was an attempt to manage the anxiety created in the now moment rather than stay with the 'anxiety and sense of being disarmed' in order for a moment of meeting to emerge. To stay with this would then mean a shift in the intersubjective field we created between us. I think Hazel was experiencing something similar and was pressing for a change in the structure of the programme. As I experienced my own anxiety, as, for example, during the executive meeting, I was struggling with the increased tension of staying in the here and now and trying to shape 'a spontaneous and authentic response to fulfil a moment of meeting'.

Which theoretical understanding one has determines how one intervenes. Interventions based on a psychoanalytic approach to anxiety involve understanding, interpreting and working through individual and organizational defences. Those based on an intersubjective perspective view anxiety as arising from potential changes in the intersubjective field leading to interventions which involve staying in the moment to co-create emergent meaning.

Finally, I wish to contrast how a complex responsive process approach (Stacey *et al.*, 2000) would understand the anxiety aroused by Ariadne. I think from this perspective anxiety is understood as a necessary part of human relating. It arises in the context of the themes which pattern interaction and changing, and in the context of power relationships which occur between people. From a complexity perspective the individual and the social are forming and being formed simultaneously by each other. The free-flowing conversation occurring between people is crucial for new patterns to emerge and creative movement to occur. Out of this conversation the themes which influence and pattern both individuals and the group develop. Often, conversations remain stuck in familiar patterns of repetitive interactions. This can be seen in the many ritualistic meetings which take place and which I was trying to avoid in the Ariadne steering group. These free-flowing conversations which occur can challenge the dominant discourse of management within the organization, which often centres on performance and output. At the same time these conversations involve the search for new meaning, and new themes emerge.

As Stacey says, 'anxiety is an inevitable companion of shifts in themes that organize the experience of relating because such shifts create uncertainty' (2000: 408). Change occurring within the organization or group is deeply felt by the individuals because it is also change for the individual. I think one can see the anxiety aroused by Ariadne as a response to shifts in themes which were patterning the process of relating. In particular, the themes of performance, output and control were giving way to new themes of participation and interaction.

At the same time, the patterns of interaction are influenced by power relations and processes of inclusion and exclusion. Stacey (2003: 130) describes how a sense of exclusion arouses anxiety, noting how attachment theory has shown the importance of the experience of attachment or inclusion for the infant to feel physiologically soothed or calmed. Without this attachment there is an experience of separation or exclusion which leads to physiological arousal experienced as anxiety. Later he says:

> The process of turn taking/turn making that reproduces and transforms themes of emergent patterns of collaboration, at the same time reproduces and transforms themes to do with inclusion and exclusion, or power, and these arouse feelings of existential anxiety, which trigger themes to deal with that anxiety in some way. The themes triggered by anxiety may well have to do with re-patterning the dynamic of inclusion and exclusion, that is, with shifting the relations of power. These and other themes triggered by anxiety may well disrupt collaboration and they may also be highly destructive. However, without such disruptions to current patterns of collaboration and power relations there could be no emergent novelty in communicative interaction and hence no novelty in any form of human interaction.
>
> (ibid.: 131)

I think this is very useful as a way to understand the reactions to Ariadne. The concern that I was disrupting a good organizational culture and leading a high-risk strategy can be understood as an anxious reaction to the shift in power relations and the disruption of current established patterns of collaboration. At the same time, through the programme a space was being allowed for free-flowing conversation out of which new themes for patterning this collaboration were emerging. From this perspective it is not surprising that anxiety was aroused; indeed, it is essential that it occurred, or no movement would have been possible. So, as I was the 'leader' in this context, my task was to try to stay with this anxiety, pay attention to and try to articulate some of the themes which were emerging. Anxiety is increased when a situation is felt to be unsafe and there is little trust between participants. At a later executive meeting

I raised this issue and expressed my appreciation that my executive colleagues were able to trust me enough to take a risk and support their staff attending the programme.

Conclusion

In this chapter I have been using my experience of setting up and facilitating a leadership development programme within my organization which draws on the ideas from complex responsive processes and group analysis. In particular, I have been illustrating the importance of leadership processes which honour the complexities of organizational life and which focus on working with the living present. It is through staying within the experience of the now and participating fully in the moment-by-moment movement which is occurring between people that those in leadership roles are best able to become effective. I am suggesting that the process of staying with the present moment arouses anxiety which has to be endured for creative movement to occur. This approach to leadership is informed from a perspective that the future is perpetually under construction, that the past is continually reconstructed in relation to the present, and that meaning arises in the present out of the continuous interactions which are occurring.

References

Bales, R. F. (1970) *Personality and Interpersonal Behavior*, New York: Holt.

Binney, G., Wilke, G., Williams, C. *et al.* (2003) *Leaders in Transition: The Dramas of Ordinary Heroes*, Berkhamsted, UK: Ashridge Publications.

Burch, N. (2004) 'Closeness and Intimacy', *British Journal of Psychotherapy* 20, 3: 361–371.

Davis, B. L., Hellervik, L. W. and Sheard, J. L. (1992) *Successful Manager's Handbook*, Minneapolis, MN: Personnel Decisions.

Fiedler, F. E. (1967) *A Theory of Leadership Effectiveness*, New York: McGraw-Hill.

Foulkes, S. H. and Anthony, E. J. ([1957] 1975) *Group Psychotherapy: The Psychoanalytic Approach*, London: Karnac.

Griffin, D. (2002) *The Emergence of Leadership: Linking Self-organization and ethics*, London: Routledge.

Hersey, P. and Blanchard, K. (1988) *Organizational Behavior*, New York: McGraw-Hill.

Kennedy, P. and Griffiths, H. (2003) 'Mental Health Collaborative Challenges Care Culture', *Psychiatric Bulletin* 27: 164–166.

Kotter, J. P. (1982) 'What Effective General Managers Really Do', *Harvard Business Review* 37: 156–167.

Mead, G. H. (1932) *The Philosophy of the Present*, New York: Prometheus Books.

Menzies Lyth, I. (1959) 'The Functioning of Social Systems as a Defense against Anxiety', in I. Menzies Lyth (1988) *Containing Anxiety in Institutions*, London: Free Association Books.

Menzies Lyth, I. (1988) *Containing Anxiety in Institutions, Selected Essays*, London: Free Association Books.

Pines, M. (1983) 'The Contribution of S. H. Foulkes to Group Therapy', in M. Pines (ed.) *The Evolution of Group Analysis*, London: Routledge.

Sarra, N. (2005) 'Organizational Development and Power Relations in an NHS Trust', unpublished thesis, University of Hertfordshire.

Shaw, P. (2002) *Changing Conversations in Organizations: A complexity approach to change*, London: Routledge.

Stacey, R. (2000) *Strategic Management and Organizational Dynamics*, 3rd edn, London: Pearson Education.

Stacey, R. (2003) *Complexity and Group Process: A radically social understanding of individuals*, London: Routledge.

Stacey, R., Griffin, D. and Shaw, P. (2000) *Complexity and Management: Fad or radical challenge to systems thinking?*, London: Routledge.

Stern, D. N. (2004) *The Present Moment in Psychotherapy and Everyday Life*, New York: W. W. Norton.

6 Complex responsive processes as a theory of organizational improvisation

Ralph Stacey

- Organizations understood as complex responsive processes of relating
- Communicative interaction
- Relations of power
- Choices arising in acts of evaluation
- The thematic patterning of human experience
- But how do strategy and planning feature in this account?

In one way or another, all the chapters in this volume have explored the fundamentally improvisational nature of ordinary, everyday life in organizations. The argument is that it is within wider improvisational processes of relating to each other that people in organizations also interact in structured, scripted ways. When organizations are written and talked about, attention is usually focused almost exclusively on emotionally detached, rational, step-by-step analysis and structured processes of planning and decision-making within monitoring forms of control. The emphasis is on predictability and the removal of uncertainty. This exclusive focus renders rationally invisible the unpredictable, emotional, responsive and spontaneous aspects of what people are doing in organizations even when they are analysing, planning and monitoring in highly rational ways. In refocusing attention on improvisation, on spontaneity and risk-taking, with the anxiety this often brings, previous chapters have referred to the theory of complex responsive processes of relating as the intellectual basis for taking such an improvisational perspective. This chapter presents a necessarily brief review of the theory of complex responsive processes.

The book series *Complexity and Emergence in Organizations* (Stacey *et al.*, 2000; Stacey, 2001; Streatfield, 2001; Fonseca, 2001; Griffin, 2001;

Shaw, 2002) provides a detailed development of the theory, and other volumes in this series explore the implications of the theory for leadership (Griffin and Stacey, 2005), global change (Stacey, 2005), public sector management (Stacey and Griffin, 2005a) and researching organizations (Stacey and Griffin, 2005b).

The theory of complex responsive processes draws on analogies from the complexity sciences, particularly the theory of complex adaptive systems. Complex adaptive systems consist of large numbers of agents, each of which interacts with some other agents. The interaction between the agents can thus be said to be local in that each agent is interacting, according to its own rules of interaction, with only a small proportion of the total population of agents. In other words, each agent is a set of rules specifying how it must interact with others, and the interaction between agents is self-organizing in that the agents are not being instructed by any other agent; each is following its own instructions. This does not amount to anarchy, because each agent cannot do whatever it likes; it must follow its rules of interaction and cannot do other than this. In this way each agent constrains and is constrained by other agents, and these constraints often conflict with each other. The properties of complex adaptive systems are explored through computer simulations (e.g. Kauffman, 1995; Ray, 1992) in which each agent is a computer program, a set of rules (digital symbols) specifying interaction with some other agents. The simulation is the iterative interaction of these agents. Large numbers of such simulations repeatedly demonstrate that such iterative, local interaction produces global patterns of order or coherence, which emerge, paradoxically predictable and unpredictable at the same time, in the absence of any global programme or plan. The conflicting constraints that the agents place on each other are essential to this emergent order. Furthermore, when these agents are different from each other, then both they and the global patterns emerging in their interaction evolve, so producing novelty (Allen, 1998a, b). So, instead of thinking that local interaction is producing a global whole, or system, we could think of patterns of local interaction as producing both further patterns of local interaction and global patterns at the same time. There is then no need to think in terms of systems or wholes. Global patterns are changing not because of some global plan, but because of local interaction. If this were to apply to human interaction it would indicate a rather profound shift in how we think about organizations. We usually think that global organizational order is the result of global plans and programmes, but from the perspective just outlined we would have to think of global organizational order as continually emerging in myriad local interactions and it would become necessary to understand the nature of such local interaction. Is there any basis for such a shift in thinking?

The simulations just referred to are highly abstract, showing the properties of certain kinds of abstract interaction between abstract agents in the domain of digital symbols. To be useful in any other domain, say biology, it is necessary to bring to these abstract relationships the attributes of that particular domain. In other words, the simulations can only ever be a source domain for analogies that might be useful in some other domain when interpreted in terms of the attributes of that other domain. In thinking about the implications of complex adaptive systems simulations for human action, it is essential, therefore, to take account of the nature of human agents. First, it is highly simplistic to think of human beings as rule-following beings. In our acting, we may take account of rules but can hardly be said to blindly follow them, as the digital agents in computer simulations do. The essential and distinctive characteristic of human agents is that they are living bodies who are conscious and self-conscious beings capable of emotion, spontaneity, imagination, fantasy and creative action. Human agents are essentially reflexive and reflective. Furthermore, they are essentially social beings in a distinctive way in that they do not interact blindly according to mechanistic rules, but engage in meaningful communicative interaction with each other in which they establish power relations between themselves. In addition, in interacting with each other, humans exercise at least some degree of choice as to how they will respond to the actions of others, and this involves the use of some form of evaluative criteria. In addition, human agents use simple and more and more complicated tools and technologies to accomplish what they choose to do. It is these embodied attributes of consciousness, self-consciousness, reflection and reflexivity, creativity, imagination and fantasy, communication, meaning, power, choice, evaluation, tool use and sociality that should be explicitly brought to any interpretation, as regards human beings, of the insights derived from complex adaptive system simulations.

As soon as one does explicitly take account of the above essential attributes of human agents, it becomes problematic to talk about human systems. Some two hundred and fifty years ago, Kant introduced the notion of system as a useful way of understanding organisms in nature, but cautioned against applying this notion to human action. A system is a whole produced by its parts and separated by a boundary from other wholes. A part is only a part in so far as it is doing what is required to produce the whole. If one thought of a human individual as a part, then by definition that individual could not exercise his or her own choices. If individuals did make their own choices, then they could not be said to be parts of a system because they would be acting in their own interests instead of in the interest of the system. In addition to making choices, humans form figurations of power relations in which they act in the interests of their own group, often in conflict with other groups. They are then acting not in the interest of a wider, more global system, but in their own joint interests. Human agents cannot, therefore, be thought of as parts of a system, because individually and collectively they exercise choices and engage in power plays. If one is to think of humans designing a system, then one encounters the problem that the designer has to be thought of as taking an observer position outside the system in order to design it. But the designer, being human, is also part of the system. Second-order systems thinking (e.g. Jackson, 2000; Midgley, 2000) tries to address this problem by widening the boundary of the system to include the observer. But this simply sets up the need for an outside observer of the wider system, so leading to an argument characterized by infinite regress.

Furthermore, with one exception, system models cannot explain how anything novel could arise, because a system is always unfolding the pattern already enfolded in it by its rules of operation. The one exception is complex adaptive systems consisting of agents characterized by diversity. Here, the model takes on a life of its own, as it were, evolving unpredictably in ways that no one has programmed. This is the same as saying that of its very essence no one can design its evolution, as small differences are amplified into significant, unforeseeable changes. The agents in such a system are forming the system while being formed by it at the same time, but in a mechanistic way in which they display no consciousness, self-consciousness, imagination, reflexivity, choice, creativity or spontaneity. Furthermore, there are practical problems with such a system model. If the model takes on a life of its own, while the phenomenon being modelled also takes on a life of its own, then it is highly unlikely that both will follow the same trajectory. The explanatory power of the model is then questionable. It also becomes unclear what might be meant by a 'boundary' or a 'whole' in relation to such a system model. If it is evolving in unpredictable ways, the 'whole' will always be incomplete and the boundary unclear. It seems to me that in pointing to the nature of their dynamics, heterogeneous complex adaptive system models begin to unravel the usefulness of thinking in systems terms at all when it comes to human action.

What then is an alternative way of thinking about the relationship between local interaction and global pattern, one that takes explicit account of the central features of human agency listed above? The alternative is to take as analogies the properties of iterative interaction, or temporal process, from the domain of heterogeneous complex adaptive systems and interpret them in terms of key human attributes. It is this approach that leads to the theory of complex responsive processes.

Organizations understood as complex responsive processes of relating

A key property of complex adaptive systems, referred to above, is that of processes of interaction in digital symbols patterning themselves as both local and global order at the same time. How might we take this abstract relationship from the domain of complex adaptive systems to the domain of human interaction? Well, human interaction is basically responsive communication between human bodies where each is conscious and self-conscious, and so capable of reflection, reflexivity, imagination and fantasy, thereby having some choice and displaying some spontaneity. To signal the move from the domain of computer simulations and systems to that of the temporal processes of human interaction, we refer to complex responsive processes instead of complex adaptive systems. The first key aspect of the complex responsive processes of relating between human bodies is communicative interaction, and George Herbert Mead's (1934) theories of conversation provide a powerful way of understanding this. It leads us to think of organizations as ongoing temporal processes of human communicative interaction.

Communicative interaction

Drawing on the work of the American pragmatist George Herbert Mead (1934), one can understand consciousness as arising in the communicative interaction between human bodies. Humans have evolved central nervous systems such that when one gestures to another, particularly in the form of vocal gesture or language, one evokes in one's own body responses to one's gesture that are similar to those evoked in other bodies. Mead refers to this as communication in the medium of significant symbols. In other words, in their acting, humans take the attitude, the tendency to act, of the other and it is because they have this capacity to communicate in significant symbols that humans can know what they are doing. It immediately follows that consciousness (knowing, mind) is a social process in which meaning emerges in the social act of gesture–response, where the gesture can never be separated from the response. Meaning does not lie in the gesture, the word, alone, but only in the gesture taken together with the response to it. Human communicative interaction is then understood as an iterative, ongoing process in which a gesture by one person, which is itself a response to a previous gesture, evokes responses in others. In this ongoing responding to each other, each is simultaneously intending a gesture and having it evoked by others. In a lifetime of interaction, people develop expectations of how others will respond to them as they try to fit in with, or diverge from, each other in their ordinary, everyday activities. Since each has the capacity for spontaneity, for surprising even themselves, none can control or be totally sure of the responses of others, and thus of the meaning which will emerge in their interactions. Human communicative interaction is thus essentially predictable and unpredictable at the same time and so involves taking risks of being misunderstood and experiencing the anxiety this brings. It is these aspects of spontaneity, simultaneous predictability and unpredictability, risk-taking and its potential for anxiety that are so characteristic of improvisational action. This is the theoretical foundation for the emphasis that previous chapters in this volume have placed on the improvisational nature of activity in organizations.

Furthermore, in communicating with each other, as the basis of everything they do, people do not simply take the attitude of the specific others with whom they are relating at any one time. Humans have the capacity for generalizing, so that when they act they always take up the attitude of what Mead called the generalized other. In other words, they always take the attitude of the group or society to their actions; they are concerned about what others might think of what they do or say. This is often unconscious and it is, of course, a powerful form of social control.

Human society is a society of selves, and selves exist only in relation to other selves. A self is an individual who organizes his or her own response by the tendencies on the part of others to respond to his or her act. Self exists in taking the role of others. According to Mead, self-consciousness is thus a social process involving the capacity humans have as subjects to take themselves as an object. This is a social process because the subject, 'I', can only ever be an object to itself as 'me', and the 'me' is one's perception of the attitude of society towards oneself. The 'I' is the often spontaneous and imaginative response of the socially formed individual to the 'me' as the gesture of society to oneself. Self is thus temporal processes, an 'I–me' dialectic, where 'I' and 'me' are inseparable phases of the same action, so that each self is socially formed while at the same time interacting selves are forming the social. Communication, then, is not simply the sending of a signal to be received by another, but rather complex social – that is, responsive – processes of self formation in which meaning and society-wide patterns emerge. One cannot, therefore, be a self independently of social interaction. Selves are social selves and society is a society of selves.

For Mead, mind is a private role play/silent conversation of a body with itself, and the social is the public, vocal interaction or conversation between bodies. Furthermore, such gestures indicate to others how the social act is likely to unfold further. Mead explains what he means by an individual calling forth a similar response in herself as in the other. He means that she is taking the attitude of the other, and he defines attitude as the tendency to act in a particular way. Mind then is the activity of experiencing a similar attitude, a similar tendency to act in a particular way, in response to gestures directed to others. Mind here is clearly a social phenomenon. In Mead's work we have a theory of consciousness and self-consciousness emerging in the social interaction between human bodies in the medium of significant symbols, and at the same time widespread social patterns also emerge. Human interaction forms and is formed by the social at the same time.

Particularly important in this way of understanding human interaction is the human capacity for generalizing, for taking the attitude of the generalized other as consciousness and the 'me' phase of the 'I–me' dialectic, where the 'me' is the generalized attitude of the society to the 'I'. Mead's main concern was not simply with a dyadic form of communication, but with much wider, much more complex patterns of interaction between many people. He was concerned with complex social acts in which many people are engaged in conversations through which they accomplish the tasks of fitting in and conflicting with each other to realize their objectives and purposes. People do not come to an interaction with each other afresh each time, because they are born into an already existing, socially evolved pattern and they continue to play their part in its further evolution. This leads Mead to his concept of the generalized other. In order to accomplish complex social acts, it is not enough for those involved to be able to take the attitude of the small numbers of people they may be directly engaged with at a particular time. They need to be able to take the attitude of all of those directly or indirectly engaged in the complex social act. It would be impossible to do this in relation to each individual so engaged, but humans have developed the capacity to generalize the attitudes of many. In acting in the present, each individual is then taking up the attitude of a few specific others and at the same time the attitude of this generalized other, the attitude of the group, the organization or the society. These wider, generalized attitudes are evolving historically and are always implicated in every human action. In play, the child takes the role of another. But in the game the child must take on the role not only of the other, but of the game; that is, of all participants in the game and its rules and procedures. The generalized other is the taking of the attitude of all other participants.

In the evolution of society many generalizations emerge which are taken up, or particularized in people's interactions with each other. This is a point of major importance. Mead draws attention to paradoxical processes of generalization and particularization at the same time. Mental and social activities are processes of generalizing and particularizing at the same time. Individuals act in relation to that which is common to all of them (generalizing) but responded to somewhat differently by each of them in each present time period (particularizing).

Mead provided a number of formulations of these generalizing–particularizing processes. One such formulation is his explanation of self-consciousness referred to earlier. In understanding self-consciousness Mead talked about a person taking the attitude of the group to himself, where that attitude is the 'me'. It is important to bear in mind that Mead was saying something more than that the self arises in the attitude, the tendency to act, of specific others towards oneself. Mead was talking about a social, generalizing process where the 'me' is a generalization across a whole community or society. For example, what it means to be an individual, a person, a man or a woman, a professional, and so on arises not in relation to a few specific people, but in relation to a particular society in a particular era. We in the West think of ourselves now as individuals in a completely different way from the way people in the West did four hundred years ago, and in a different way from people in other cultures. In the 'I–me' dialectic, then, we have a process in which the generalization of the 'me' is made particular in the response of the 'I' for a particular person at a particular time in a particular place. For example, I may take up what it means to be a man in my society in a particular way that differs in some respects from how others see themselves as men in my own society, in other societies and at other times.

Mead's discussion of what he called the social object is yet another formulation of this generalizing and particularizing process. Mead distinguishes between a physical object and a social object. A physical object exists in nature and is the proper object of study in the natural sciences, while the social object is the proper object of study in the social sciences. While the physical object can be understood in terms of itself, the social object has to be understood in terms of social acts. Mead referred to market exchange as an example of a social act. When one person offers to buy food, this act obviously involves a complex range of responses from other people to provide the food. However, it involves more than this, because the one making the offer can only know how to make the offer if he or she is able to take the attitude of the other parties to the bargain. All essential phases of the complex social act of exchange must appear in the actions of all involved and appear as essential features of each individual's actions. Buying and selling are involved in each other.

Mead, therefore, defined the social act as one involving the cooperation of many people in which the different parts of the act undertaken by different individuals appear in the act of each individual. The tendencies to act as others act are present in the conduct of each individual involved, and it is this presence that is responsible for the appearance of the social object in the experience of each individual. The social act defines the object of the act, and this is a social object which is only to be found in the conduct of the different individuals engaged in the complex social act. The social object appears in the experience of each individual as a stimulus to a response not only by that individual, but also by the others involved; this is how each can know how the others are likely to act, and it is the basis of coordination. A social object is thus a kind of gesture together with tendencies to respond in particular ways. Social objects are common plans or patterns of action related to the existent future of the act. The social object is a generalization which is taken up, or particularized, by all in a group/society in their actions. Social objects have evolved in the history of the society of selves and each individual is born into such a world of social objects. The conduct of individuals marks out and defines the social objects which make up their environment in which the nature of the social objects and the sensitivities of individuals answer to each other. In other words, individuals are forming social objects while being formed by them in an evolutionary process.

Mead linked social objects to social control. Social control is the bringing of the act of the individual into relation with the social object, and the contours of the object determine the organization of the act. The social act is distributed among many, but the whole social object appears in the experience of all of them. Social control depends upon the degree to which the individual takes the attitude of the others – that is, takes the attitude which is the social object. All institutions are social objects and serve to control individuals who find them in their experience.

It is important to note here how the generalizations, the social objects referred to earlier, are only to be found in the way in which they are being made particular at any one time in any one contingent situation. People are continually interpreting and negotiating with each other the meaning of the generalizations that have emerged and continue to evolve in the myriad ongoing local interactions between people. This continual interpretation and negotiation in local situations involves responsiveness, imagination, spontaneity and all the other aspects of improvisational activity, so providing a complex, richer theoretical foundation for the arguments developed in previous chapters of this book.

Mead also linked social objects to values, and in another formulation of the interaction between the general and the particular, he draws a distinction between cult values and their functionalization. Cult values are idealizations that emerge in the evolution of a society. Mead said that they were the most precious part of our heritage. Examples of cult values are democracy, treating others with respect, regarding life as sacred, belief in being American or British, and so on. Other examples are mission and vision statements in organizations. Such cult values present people with the image of an idealized future shorn of all constraints. If such values are applied directly to action, without allowing for variations contingent on a specific situation, then those undertaking such action form a cult in which they exclude all who do not comply. In the usual course of events, however, this does not happen, as people act on present interpretations of cult values. For example, a cult value to do with the sacredness of life is not directly applied in some places, leading to conflict regarding, for example, abortion. Functionalization of cult values inevitably leads to conflict and the negotiation of compromises around such conflict. Functionalizing of values is the enactment of values in the ordinary, local interactions between people in the living present. In his notion of cult values, Mead points not only to the generalizing tendencies of interacting people, but also to the idealizing tendencies characteristic of their interaction. Such idealizations may be good or bad depending upon who is doing the judging. Mead's notions of social objects and cult values have something in common with the notions of social structure, habit and routine. What is distinctive about Mead's approach to these matters, however, is how he avoided positing social structure as a phenomenon that exists outside individuals. Social objects and cult values are generalizations and idealizations that only have any existence in their particularization in the ordinary, everyday interactions between people in the living present. What is happening as people try to functionalize cult values is processes of interpretation and negotiation which always carry the potential for spontaneity, the properties of predictability and unpredictability characteristic of improvisational activity. Once again Mead's perspective on values provides a theoretical foundation for taking an improvisational approach to understanding life in organizations.

The second key aspect of complex responsive processes of relating has to do with power. Here the work of Norbert Elias is particularly instructive.

Relations of power

Drawing on the work of Elias ([1939] 2000), one understands how the processes of communicative interacting constitute relations of power. For Elias, power is not something anyone possesses, but, rather, is a characteristic of all human relating. In order to form, and stay in, a relationship with someone else, one cannot do whatever one wants. As soon as we enter into relationships, therefore, we constrain and are constrained by others, and, of course, we also enable and are enabled by others. There is a clear analogy with the conflicting constraints characteristic of the complex adaptive system simulations described earlier in this chapter. In human action, power is this enabling–constraining relationship where the power balance is tilted in favour of some and against others, depending on the relative need they have for each other. For example, one may have control over resources that others need. Elias showed how such power relationships form figurations, or groupings, in which some are included and others are excluded, and where the power balance is tilted in favour of some groupings and against others. These groupings establish powerful feelings of belonging which constitute each individual's 'we' identity. These 'we' identities, derived from the groups we belong to, are inseparable from each of our 'I' identities. As with Mead, then, we can see that processes of human relating form and are formed by individual and collective identities, which inevitably reflect complex, conflictual and cooperative patterns of power relating. Furthermore, Elias shows how these power figurations are sustained, unconsciously, by ideologies, which are in turn sustained by gossip and processes of shame. Power relations are always made to feel natural by an unconscious underlying ideology. It is this that sustains the dominant discourse of a group, which of course is reflected in patterns of power relating.

Elias's approach to power links well with Mead's notion of communicative interaction. Social object/cult value both constrain and enable mind/self and interaction (social). Another way of talking about power, then, is to talk about the enabling/constraining nature of social object and cult value as they are particularized and functionalized in local interaction in specific contingent situations. But just what form do these enabling constraints take? Some aspects are as follows:

- People form groups and they label or name such groupings. In so doing, they differentiate themselves from others in an 'us' and 'them' dynamic. We can therefore describe processes of power, of enabling and constraining, in terms of the dynamics of inclusion–exclusion and the formation of identity in local interaction in contingent situations.
- Enabling and constraining can also be understood as activities of cooperating and competing, and this immediately directs attention to the motivations of altruism and self-centredness or rivalry, driven by the desire to retain and strengthen identity and belonging. The rivalry is frequently around which discourse is to dominate, and about control of resources too.
- The emotions of shame, envy and jealousy as well as empathy, compassion and acceptance also help to explain the manner in which people constrain and enable each other.
- Fantasy and imagination as well as acting and thinking in defensive ways (social and individual) are also ways of describing the enabling and constraining activities of relating.
- We can describe enabling and constraining activities in terms of politics and negotiation processes and the often conflicting ideologies underlying these processes.
- Throughout, we are talking about cooperation and conflict and how they are dealt with. For Mead, conflict is intrinsic to particularizing, functionalizing processes.

When we talk about complex responsive processes of relating, therefore, we are talking about the complex emotions and motivations, as well as the spontaneity and imagination which characterize ordinary, everyday communicating and power relating in organizations. What I have been describing is the complex, improvisational nature of human relating, so pointing to the theoretical basis for claiming that organizational life is improvisational.

Choices arising in acts of evaluation

In their communicative interacting and power relating, humans are always making choices between one action and another. This may be on the basis of conscious desires and intentions, or unconscious desires and choices – for example, those that are habitual, impulsive, obsessive or compulsive. In other words, human action is always evaluative, sometimes consciously and at other times unconsciously. The criteria for evaluating these choices are values and norms, together constituting ideology. This aspect is explored more fully in chapter 2 of another volume in this series of books (Griffin and Stacey, 2005).

Norms (morals, the right, the 'ought') are evaluative criteria taking the form of obligatory restrictions which have emerged as generalizations and become habitual in a history of social interaction (Joas, 2000). We are all socialized to take up the norms of the particular groups and the society to which we belong, and this restricts what we can do as we particularize the generalized norms in our moment-by-moment specific action situations. Elias's work shows in detail how norms constitute major aspects of the personality structures, or identities, of interdependent people. *Values* (ethics, the 'good') are individually felt voluntary compulsions to choose one desire, action, or norm rather than another. Values arise in social processes of self formation and self transcendence (Dewey, 1934; Joas, 2000) – they are fundamental aspects of self, giving meaning to life, opening up opportunities for action. They arise in intense interactive experiences which are seized by the imagination and idealized as some 'whole' to which people then feel strongly committed. Mead (1938) described these as cult values, which need to be functionalized in particular contingent situations, and this inevitably involves conflict. Together the voluntary compulsion of values and the obligatory restriction of norms constitute *ideology*. Ideology is the basis on which people choose desires and actions, and it unconsciously sustains power relations by making a particular figuration of power feel natural (Dalal, 1998). We can see, then, that complex responsive processes of human relating form and are formed by values, norms and ideologies as integral aspects of self/identity formation in its simultaneously individual and collective form.

Evaluative choice is another way of talking about decision-making. Decision-making is usually described as a step-by-step, linear, rational process, conducted by autonomous individuals but also sometimes in teams following clear, rational decision-making procedures. Here the rational is split from the emotional, which is usually thought to interfere with rational decision-making. However, recent brain research (Damasio, 1994, 1999) shows that the same areas of the brain deal with emotion and the selection of rational courses of action. Feelings and emotions act as important selectors of appropriate courses of action. Purely rational decision-making is thus impossible, and what we describe as rational decision-making in ordinary organizational life is always embedded in feelings and emotion. We come, then, to understand decision-making in terms of emotional, ideological, social process of communicative interaction and power relating, rather than in terms of the thinking activity of the rational, autonomous individual. Decision-making is thus characterized by the spontaneous, risk-taking, anxiety-provoking improvisational activity that has been explored in previous chapters of this volume.

The thematic patterning of human experience

In the above description of the fundamental aspects of the complex responsive processes of human relating, I have referred to *patterns* of communicative interaction and *figurations* of power relations. These patterns and figurations can be understood as themes, taking both propositional and narrative forms, which emerge and re-emerge in the iteration, in each succeeding present, of the interactive processes of communication, power and evaluation. Values, norms and ideologies are examples of such themes. These themes organize the experience of being together.

Complex responsive processes of relating are, therefore, simultaneously processes of communicative interaction, power relating and ideological evaluation in which local individual selves/identities and the global patterns of the social emerge at the same time, each forming and being formed by the other at the same time. They are continually iterated as continuity and transformation, which is possible because of the spontaneity of the 'I' and the possibility of small differences being escalated into transformed patterns. And pattern means the largely narrative themes that are individual selves and social phenomena at the same time. All this can usefully be understood as improvisational activity, which is certainly not haphazard, impulsive or thoughtless activity, but highly complex, skilled performances of interdependent people.

But how do strategy and planning feature in this account?

In the literature on organizations, and in the way managers in organizations talk, strategic planning means deciding on some kind of global outcome for some long-term period, say five years. This is thought first and action later, thought before action. The plan or design is the 'thought' and the implementation is the 'action'. The assumption, then, is that it is possible to design global patterns well before they are realized, and this in turn implies that it is possible to predict the outcomes of action to a useful degree. Local interaction is then understood as the process of implementing the plan or design. This is the essence of the planning and design schools of strategic management in the literature, it is how managers think and talk in business organizations, and it is what governments have imported from business as the basis of centralized, managerialist forms of public sector governance (see another volume in this series: Stacey and Griffin, 2005b). A number of writers and practitioners have been critical of this approach for some time, one such prominent writer being Mintzberg (Mintzberg *et al.*, 1998). Mintzberg and others favour another school of strategy in which organizations learn their way into the future, and they distinguish between deliberate and emergent strategy. The emphasis shifts from planning to processes of learning. Senge (1990) is a key writer here and he identifies five disciplines of the learning organization: systems thinking, mental models, visions, personal mastery and team working. He claims that organizations develop according to a limited number of general archetypes and that systems thinking allows managers to identify leverage points in organizations and then operate on them to shift from a dysfunctional archetype. So here too we get the idea that global patterns can be identified beforehand and changed directly through operating at leverage points. Local interaction then becomes working in teams to learn, and so shift individual mental models and global archetypes. In both cases the focus of attention is on the global and long term, and it is thought possible to operate directly on the global in some way so as to actualize prior intention regarding the global.

A complex responsive processes perspective emphasizes the unpredictability of long-term outcomes/patterns, holding that design and planning with regard to the global can only achieve what they claim to achieve with regard to short-term, repetitive and thus reasonably predictable activity. Even then, any plans, designs, visions, descriptions of archetypes are simply articulations of global generalizations/idealizations and these articulations have to be made particular in each specific, contingent situation, which leads to conflict that must be negotiated. The articulation of the global generalization is an abstraction from experience and can only be found in the experience of particularizing the generalization and functionalizing the idealization. So even with regard to the short-term and rather repetitive events, planning activities will be problematic, although I would say that in such restricted situations they remain useful, budgeting being an example. Central to the complex responsive process perspective is the notion of emergence, according to which global patterns continually emerge in local interaction, and this means that they come about in the absence of global plans or designs, or, if there are such global plans and designs, they will not be operating as the cause of the global pattern that appears, because that global pattern is emergent. So, in these circumstances, any strategic planning, organizational leverage activities are largely fantasies whose function might largely be to form social defences against anxiety. The problem with them as a defence is that they blinker people and if taken seriously can easily get in the way of more improvisational, spontaneous behaviour. So, it is my view that such activities are, in many ways, a distracting waste of time and could be discontinued with the benefits far outweighing any drawbacks. Instead of being planned, global patterns emerge in myriad local interactions, and this is especially true for global patterns displaying any form of novelty. It becomes extremely important, then, to understand the largely improvisational nature of such ordinary local interaction. This does not mean that people are acting without intention or expectation. Those engaged in local interactions do have intentions, perhaps even plans, for their own local interaction, but the global patterns emerge in the interplay between all of their intentions/plans, and the interplay cannot be said to be planned, so neither can the global pattern. Instead, local interaction takes on the form of improvisational acting with a high degree of spontaneity. Such improvisation/spontaneous acting cannot be said to be planning, although it does not mean that there is no intention on the part of those engaging in the improvisational local interaction. The relationship between the local and the global is explored in some detail in another volume in this series (Stacey, 2005).

References

Allen, P. M. (1998a) 'Evolving Complexity in Social Science', in G. Altman and W. A. Koch (eds) *Systems: New Paradigms for the Human Sciences*, New York: Walter de Gruyter.

Allen, P. M. (1998b) 'Modeling Complex Economic Evolution', in F. Schweitzer and G. Silverberg (eds) *Selbstorganization*, Berlin: Dunker und Humbolt.

Dalal, F. (1998) *Taking the Group Seriously: Towards a post-Foulkesian group analytic theory*, London: Jessica Kingsley.

Damasio, A. R. (1994) *Descartes' Error: Emotion, reason and the human brain*, London: Picador.

Damasio, A. R. (1999) *The Feeling of What Happens: Body and emotion in the making of consciousness*, London: Heinemann.

Dewey, J. (1934) *A Common Faith*, New Haven, CT: Yale University Press.

Elias, N. ([1939] 2000) *The Civilizing Process*, Oxford: Blackwell.

Fonseca, J. (2001) *Complexity and Innovation in Organizations*, London: Routledge.

Griffin, D. (2001) *The Emergence of Leadership: Linking Self-organization and ethics*, London: Routledge.

Griffin, D. and Stacey, R. (eds) (2005) *Complexity and the Experience of Leading Organizations*, London: Routledge.

Jackson, M. C. (2000) *Systems Approaches to Management*, New York: Kluwer.

Joas, H. (2000) *The Genesis of Values*, Cambridge: Polity Press.

Kauffman, S. A. (1995) *At Home in the Universe*, New York: Oxford University Press.

Mead, G. H. (1934) *Mind, Self and Society*, Chicago, IL: University of Chicago Press.

Mead, G. H. (1938) *The Philosophy of the Present*, Chicago, IL: University of Chicago Press.

Midgley, G. (2000) *Systemic Intervention: Philosophy, methodology, and practice*, New York: Kluwer.

Mintzberg, H., Ahlstrand, B. and Lampel, J. (1998) *Strategy Safari: A guide through the wilds of strategic management*, New York: Free Press.

Ray, T. S. (1992) 'An Approach to the Synthesis of Life', in G. C. Langton, C. Taylor, J. Doyne-Farmer and S. Rasmussen (eds) *Artificial Life II, Santa Fe Institute*, Studies in the Sciences of Complexity, vol. 10, Reading, MA: Addison-Wesley.

Senge, P. M. (1990) *The Fifth Discipline: The art of practice of the learning organization*, New York: Doubleday.

Shaw, P. (2002) *Changing Conversations in Organizations: A complexity approach to change*, London: Routledge.

Stacey, R. (2001) *Complex Responsive Processes in Organizations: Learning and knowledge creation*, London: Routledge.

Stacey, R. (2005) *Experiencing Emergence in Organizations: Local interaction and the emergence of global pattern*, London: Routledge.

Stacey, R. and Griffin, D. (2005a) *A Complexity Perspective on Researching Organizations: Taking experience seriously*, London: Routledge.

Stacey, R. and Griffin, D. (2005b) *Complexity and the Experience of Managing in Public Sector Organizations*, London: Routledge.

Stacey, R., Griffin, D. and Shaw, P. (2000) *Complexity and Management: Fad or radical challenge to systems thinking?*, London: Routledge.

Streatfield, P. (2001) *The Paradox of Control in Organizations*, London: Routledge.

Index

Printed in the United Kingdom
by Lightning Source UK Ltd.
116356UKS00004B/17